The Wedding Video Handbook

The Wedding Video Handbook

How to Succeed in the Wedding Video Business

Kirk Barber

San Francisco, CA

Published by CMP Books
an imprint of CMP Media LLC
600 Harrison Street, San Francisco, CA 94107 USA
Tel: 415-947-6615; Fax: 415-947-6015

www.cmpbooks.com
email: books@cmp.com

Managing editor: Gail Saari
Layout design: Michael Cutter
Cover design: David Hamamoto

Distributed to the book trade in the U.S. by:
Publishers Group West
1700 Fourth Street
Berkeley, CA 94710
1-800-788-3123

Distributed in Canada by:
Jaguar Book Group
100 Armstrong Avenue
Georgetown, Ontario M6K 3E7 Canada
905-877-4483

For individual orders and for information on special discounts for quantity orders, please contact:
CMP Books Distribution Center, 6600 Silacci Way, Gilroy, CA 95020
Tel: 1-800-500-6875 or 408-848-3854; fax: 408-848-5784
Email: cmp@rushorder.com; Web: www.cmpbooks.com

Printed in the United States of America
05 06 07 08 09   5 4 3 2 1

ISBN: 1-57820-281-7

CMP*Books*

Contents

Making Money Enriching Lives

Congratulations on your decision to become a wedding videographer! You are about to join thousands of creative artists who enhance the lives of hundreds of thousands of people around the world while enjoying all of the benefits of working for themselves. You may be wondering how someone with a video camera can enrich other people's lives.

Every week of every year thousands of couples around the world get married. Many of these ceremonies are followed by celebrations with family and friends. Weddings are considered to be one of the happiest (if not the happiest) times of their lives. It provides an opportunity to reunite with loved ones near and far. It represents the beginning of a new chapter in their lives, a time to celebrate the passage from being a child in one family to becoming a husband or wife and beginning a new family.

For many couples, this may be the last time they'll get to see their grandparents, aunts, uncles, or even their own parents. Since it is a time for celebration, you'll often witness many of the guests truly enjoying themselves. Weddings create a tremendous opportunity to capture the magic and emotion of these special moments. The video footage recorded by a wedding videographer is priceless.

The Power of Video

Modern technology not only allows us to record these moments but also to creatively weave them into a unique, cinematically dramatic keepsake for families to enjoy for generations to come. The addition of wedding video made possible for the first time the ability for children to see what really happened at their parents' wedding. They get to see relatives they may have never met. Video allows them to share a special memory with their parents.

Anyone who has ever had a traditional wedding and reception can tell you that for the many months of planning that went into it, the wedding day sure goes by really fast. Over the years, I've spoken with many of my wedding clients after their wedding day, and they confirmed that not only did the day go by fast but also that they were having difficulty remembering a lot of it. They often describe the day as a blur. While watching their own video, a few brides admit they didn't remember certain portions of the event and even some of the activities that the video clearly showed them participating in.

Even though photography has been around for more than a century, nothing can capture the essence or emotion of a wedding celebration quite like video. And, photography doesn't capture the sounds from that day. They can laugh all over again at the best man's toast or wipe the dampness from their eyes as they watch the bride's dad share a special dance with his daughter. Through video, couples can relive any part of their wedding day anytime they wish and never forget this day.

The Need for Video

The recent tragedies over the past several years, from 9/11 to wildfires to hurricanes, have demonstrated why videos of special occasions are more important now than ever before. Videos preserve precious memories from those special times with family and friends. Most people will agree that their most valuable belongings are their photos, videos, and memories. Photos show how someone looked, video shows what they were really like.

Creative and Rewarding

This is where you, the videographer, come in. Using your captivating methods of documenting this momentous event and artistically editing the video footage, you'll be able to create compelling storytelling videos that will be cherished for many years and generations. Well-produced videos usually receive gratuitous compliments and thank-yous from very grateful clients.

In addition to receiving many accolades, you can generate income with your creativity while working from the comfort of your own home. Most wedding videographers still operate their businesses from their homes either on a part-time or full-time basis. Even though you may have to commit yourself to working some Saturdays, you can adjust the rest of the work around your schedule. The level of creativity commonly used in wedding videos will allow your imagination to soar.

Of all the benefits I've discussed so far, my favorite is when my clients look me in the eye and offer a warm, sincere, heartfelt, "Thank you very much for the work you've done for us." This is worth far more to me than all of the money I've earned from this business.

Every Business Has Its Challenges

If you've ever attempted to start a business before or know anyone who has, you know how challenging it can be. There's a lot to learn about the process of getting your business started and running successfully. Over the years, I've watched many people buy a camera and tripod, get some business cards, and call themselves professional wedding videographers. Here's what I have discovered: The ones who continue to learn their craft always seem to have plenty of clients; the ones who don't are lucky if they survive longer than five years in the business.

There are challenges specific to this business. You have to learn about many different types of electronic equipment, what to buy and how to use it. As with any business, you need to understand how to use marketing and advertising to attract customers to your business. You should know how to talk to potential customers and how to turn them into clients. Then there are the actual procedures for videotaping and editing a wedding video. And, finally, learning how to burn, label, and package a DVD.

I have to be honest with you—the odds are against new business.

The bad news:

· 50 percent of new businesses fail within the first year.
· 95 percent of new businesses fail within the first three years.

Most business failures are due to the business owner's lack of knowledge about how to run a business and their inability to seek outside assistance or advice.

The good news: Studies on entrepreneurs who have had training or education in entrepreneurial skills consistently show a higher success rate, as much as 80 to 90 percent.

The fact that you've picked up this book means you're on the right path.

The Road to Success

When my wife and I moved to San Diego—one of the most expensive places to live in America—we had no jobs, no contacts, and very little money. I knew nothing about wedding videos or running a business. I was forced to learn everything I could as fast as possible or face bankruptcy soon. I took out a loan on my car and leased some equipment to get started. Within 18 months I had videotaped 28 weddings and booked over 10 more. My unique approach to doing things has made me a leader in the industry.

This book contains over nine years' worth of experience and inside secrets that many of today's wedding videographers don't even know. Within these pages, you'll learn everything you need to know to get your business off the ground quickly, including setting up your business, choosing the right equipment, marketing, videotaping, editing, and packaging your videos. I'll show you how to avoid some of the biggest mistakes that can kill a business, and I'll teach you techniques that can propel you past many of your competitors within your first two years in business.

Are you ready to begin your new career? Then, let's not waste anymore time; let's get started.

Chapter 1

Setting Up Your Business

Welcome to your new venture. Starting a new business can be a very exciting time in your life. Whether this is your first business or not, try to enjoy the journey you're about to embark on. The first step is to come up with a name for your business that is unique and fits your personality.

Choosing a Name

The name you decide to use needs to be unique, meaning that no one else in your area is using it. It should be a name that goes with your personality, but it needs to sound professional. For example, I would suggest staying away from a name like "Joey's Videotaping Service." You need a name that would make a client confident in hiring you. You have two options for choosing a name—you may use your own name or create a fictitious name. I'll cover the pros and cons of each in a moment.

Fictitious Name

A fictitious name is the legal description for a name for your business that you have made up and does not include your actual name. An example of a fictitious name would be "Peak Video Services." Before you can use a specific name, you will need to search your local government's listings of fictitious names to verify that no one else is currently using it. Once you've confirmed that your company name is not being used elsewhere in the county, you may then record your fictitious name application with the county clerk or recorder.

Fictitious Name Document

If you want to name your company "Videos 'R Us," for example, every state or county in the U.S. may require you to file a fictitious name document that simply states that you will be doing business as (DBA) Videos 'R Us. I recommend that you first check with your county clerk or government office for more information about how to file this document.

Pros and Cons of Each Name Type

Here are a few of the pros and cons for each type of business name:

1) Using your own name.

Benefits:

- It's easy to remember.
- Everyone knows who owns the business. If they remember your name, they'll remember the business' name.
- It may project an image of personalized service to your customers.
- You don't have to file a fictitious name form.

Disadvantages:

- Everyone knows who owns the business. More on this in a moment.
- It could make the business harder to transition to a new owner should you decide to sell it in the future.
- It may project a less professional image than those of your competitors.

2) Using a fictitious name.

Benefits:

- It's easier to transition to a new owner if you decide to sell the business at a later time.
- It projects a more professional image.
- It offers more creative possibilities for developing a logo.

Disadvantages:

- You'll have to file a fictitious name form at regular intervals.

Let's say you've decided to use your own name, for example, John Smith Video Productions. If your customers can remember your name then they should be able to remember your company's name. For example, when people do business with a company named Al's Auto Repair, it may give them the feeling that they're more likely to receive personalized service, and they may feel more at ease, particularly if they mainly speak with Al. If Al is never available to talk with the customers, then it may not mean as much to them. Years later, should Al decide he'd like to sell his business, the new owner may not want to own Al's Auto Service, especially if her name is Terri. There is a nice benefit to this option in that you'll never have to worry about filing a fictitious name statement.

IMPORTANT TIP You should check with your county government offices to verify their specific requirements. Filing a fictitious name statement does not prevent anyone else from using that name in other counties. If you desire to have true exclusivity of the use of your name you'll need to file a trademark or similar document with the U.S. government. Consult a patent, copyright, and trademark expert for information on how to do this. These guidelines refer to setting up a business in the United States only. Outside the U.S., consult your local government agencies for the proper procedures.

There are some disadvantages to this option, one being that sometimes people perceive a company with a name like Citywide Video Productions to be more established and reputable than Hal's Video Productions. This brings us to your first marketing lesson: Think like your customer. How would *you* respond to the name? Another problem could arise if you ever have a bad experience with a customer. For example, what if there was a major problem with their video? Since they worked with you most of the time, they're more likely to remember your (and your company's) name when they tell their friends about their bad experience. This is a minor issue but it may be worth considering.

Now, on to the fictitious names. It may take you a few attempts to come up with a fictitious name that hasn't already been taken. County governments may require you to refile your fictitious name statement every few years or so or if your business moves to a new location. Check with your local government regarding their policies regarding when you will need to refile.

On the plus side, in the previous example, Terri is not likely to have any objection to taking over a business called Integrity Auto Repair, particularly if the company has a good reputation among its customers. The name "Integrity" seems more trustworthy than "Al's," therefore portraying a more professional image. A fictional name for your company may also provide more creative freedom when it comes to designing a logo for your company. How do you come up with a logo for Al?

Create a Logo

I strongly recommend having a well-designed logo for your business. You may want to seek the assistance of a graphic designer. A good logo will help keep your company's name or image in your customers' minds. For example, when someone mentions the "golden arches," what do you think of? During my first couple of years in business, I had several people tell me, "I've heard of your company before." The only advertising we were doing at the time was in the Yellow Pages. I don't know too many people who regularly read the Yellow Pages, but our logo did contain a recognizable design.

Obtaining Licenses, Permits, and Insurance

Once you've settled on the name for your business, it will be time to obtain the necessary permits and licenses to make you legal.

Business License

You'll need to check with your local city and county governments to determine if you need to have a business license. Many will require one before you can legally conduct business within their jurisdiction. These licenses usually are not very expensive, and customers will trust you more when you mention that you're a licensed business.

Reseller's Permit

Many state and local governments may require you to charge sales tax on the videos you produce. Many have argued that wedding videographers are providing a service and should not be required to collect sales tax. The state of California, as of this writing, does not see it that way. California views wedding videos as a tangible product and subject to sales tax. Others might argue that only the price of the actual videotape or DVD should be subject to sales tax, not the labor portion. The tax board treats the sales tax on videos much like the sales tax on automobiles. Automobiles are taxed based on the full sales price of the vehicle, which includes the labor that went into making it. The

State of California claims that the actual video being handed over to the client is a tangible product and that all of the labor that went into producing it is taxable, just as with the automobile.

If your government requires you to pay the sales tax, you will need to apply for a reseller's permit. Contact your local and state governments regarding their policies and procedures. Usually, it's a pretty simple process. They'll ask you a few questions and send you a document with an identification number on it. This ID number will often be referred to as your reseller number. You will need to keep the reseller's permit, and you may be required to display it at your place of business. There is a bright side to having a reseller's permit—you may be entitled to waive any sales tax you would normally have to pay when you purchase the supplies necessary for producing your videos, such as blank videotapes and DVDs.

Insurance

If you want to keep your business, I'd advise you to have all of the appropriate types of insurance.

Liability Insurance

I strongly encourage you to purchase liability insurance. Liability insurance covers you for any damages caused as a result of your business conducting activities relating to the production of videos. For example, if one of your pieces of equipment were to fall over and injure someone or cause damage to the premises when you are videotaping, your insurance would handle the claim, as your company is ultimately responsible.

Some business liability insurance policies may also cover any equipment that may get stolen from your place of business or where you happen to be videotaping. There have been many reports recently of video cameras being stolen at weddings. All it takes is to set down the camera for a few moments while you go into another room to check on something and, when you come back, it's gone.

Errors and Omissions Insurance

There is another type of insurance called Errors and Omissions (E&O) insurance. This type of insurance works in addition to the liability insurance and protects you against what I call circumstances beyond your control. Although it is not a common occurrence, there have been times when a videographer inadvertently missed a key moment while videotaping a wedding, for one reason or another. Some examples of this are when the video camera jams or malfunctions, causing some or all of the picture or sound to not be recorded or not recorded properly. Another instance may be a simple operator error that causes you to miss the bride's bouquet toss. In Chapter 16, I'll discuss some ways of handling these types of situations. If any of these were to happen to you and the bride decided to sue you over it, the E&O insurance company would handle the case. It's definitely worth the piece of mind.

Setting Up Your Office

I will start this section discussing whether you should rent office space or run your business out of your home. Unless you have a lot of money for starting your business, you may want to try working from home. There is a significant amount of overhead costs involved with renting an office space. As you're getting started, you should save as much money as you can so you'll have more to market your business with. However, if there is consistently too much chaos in your home (kids running around, toys everywhere, people yelling and screaming) then you may have to consider renting office space. I'll talk more about creating a professional image for your business in Chapter 6, Marketing and Getting the Clients.

Tax Deductions for the Office

Most of the expenses involved in renting office space are tax-deductible. If you are able to dedicate a specific portion of your home for your business only, there are some tax deductions here as well. You should consult your tax advisor regarding tax benefits for either of these options.

Renting Office Space

If you choose to rent an office, make sure you have enough room for an administrative desk and a demo area to show videos to prospective clients.

You'll also want to have another room to put your editing equipment in to keep it separate from the demo area. You should be able to get by with an office space of 300 to 400 square feet. Make sure the entrance and demo areas are kept clean and neat at all times. You never know when a client will drop by. When a customer walks in, the room should look like a professional environment that will instill confidence and encourage your prospective customers to trust you.

Working From Home

If you decide to run your business from home, you have two choices on where to meet clients, at your home or theirs. I'll talk about where you should meet them in Chapter 7, Phone Calls and Appointments. If you want to meet them at your home, you will need to follow much of the advice in the previous paragraph. Keep the kids, the toys, and the clutter away from the entrance and demo areas that your prospective clients will be in.

Office Equipment

The equipment you will need for editing videos (such as computers and monitors) will be discussed in the next chapter. Right now, we're talking about setting up the part of your business that will help you keep track of your customers and the administrative portion of your business. These recommendations will apply regardless of where you set up your office.

I suggest getting an office desk for administrative use if you don't already have one. A desk with two file drawers is preferred so you can file customer contracts and invoices that you may need to refer to later. As your business grows, you'll need to add a separate file cabinet, but for now a simple office desk with file drawers will suffice. Office supply stores like Staples or Office Depot sell desks for around $200 to $300. There are also office furniture stores that sell higher-quality used desks and chairs for around the same price. Don't forget the chair.

A telephone, calculator, and fax machine are necessities. You never know when a client is going to want to fax you a contract to hire you. I strongly encourage that you have a computer that is separate from the computer you plan to edit with. This computer should be used for handling customer invoices, creating contracts, working on marketing materials, drafting letters to prospective clients, Internet access, and so on. You can buy computers for this purpose for less than $500 now. They can save you hours of bookkeeping hassles.

Computer Software

I recommend that you get a bookkeeping software program like QuickBooks, Peachtree, or other accounting programs to help you keep track of your invoices (income) and bills (expenses). I have been using QuickBooks and feel it fulfills every need I have at this time. I have not used Peachtree so, I cannot offer any more information on it. Check out several of them, if you prefer, to find the one you like the best. I also suggest getting a word processing program and a spreadsheet program. Microsoft Office contains both of these and there are others, as well. You'll need the word processing for generating letters to clients or prospective clients. It may also come in handy for writing contracts.

Internet service

I definitely recommend signing up for Internet service if you don't already have it. Today's business world demands email accessibility. Currently, a majority of my clients find me through my web site. You can get dial-up Internet service for as low as $10 a month, but DSL or a cable modem is preferred.

Phone Service

A cellular phone is not essential to get your business started but it may be helpful. Obtaining a separate phone line for your business is crucial. You don't want to be losing customers while someone in your household ties up your personal phone line talking to a friend. Your new business phone number is the one you'll be putting on your business cards, flyers, brochures, web site, and any other piece of promotional material you decide to distribute. When I first started my company, I used our residence phone line as my fax line and outgoing phone call line so I could keep the business line free for incoming calls from prospective clients.

Business Cards

Business cards are a must. Have them made up as soon as possible. I'll discuss brochures in Chapter 6.

Now that your business is set up and ready to go, it's time to buy your video equipment.

Chapter 2
Choosing Video Equipment

Once you've taken the necessary steps for setting up your business, it's time to begin purchasing or leasing your equipment. There is quite a variety of audio and video equipment to choose from in all price ranges. The biggest challenge you'll face in this endeavor is determining which production tools best fit your situation, budget, and desired results.

Equipment for Videotaping

Video Cameras

When you begin looking at cameras, you'll be hearing terms like single-chip, three-chip, quarter-inch chips, third-inch chips, half-inch chips, DV, miniDV, Digital8, Betacam, DVCAM, DVCPRO, and more. Many of these terms refer to the capabilities of the cameras and the media format each camera uses for recording. I'll go over each of these terms in a moment.

Video cameras, or camcorders as they are often referred to, can be classified into three categories: full-sized industrial, mid-sized prosumer, and mini to small-sized consumer.

Professional

The full-sized, industrial cameras are like the ones you typically see used by television news teams (sometimes referred to as broadcast). Camera operators often

VIDEO TERM The term "prosumer" was created to describe a category of electronic equipment between professional equipment used by television broadcasters and large production companies and consumer equipment sold in most consumer electronics stores. Most of the major electronics manufacturers like Sony and Panasonic have two separate divisions of their companies that are responsible for developing equipment for the broadcast and consumer markets. Often, the top-of-the-line consumer products and/or the entry-level broadcast products are referred to as prosumer products.

shoot with these by placing the back half of the camera on their shoulder with their right hand supporting the lens and front of the camera. Full-sized cameras offer the best picture quality, but they can weigh from 11 to 35 pounds when equipped with lights, batteries, and other accessories. These cameras usually come with three-chip technology. High-definition (HD or HDCAM), Betacam, Digital Betacam, DV, DVCAM, and DVCPRO are examples of videotape formats commonly used in these types of cameras. The prices for these cameras start at $5,000.

Consumer

Small-sized consumer cameras are like the ones sold at consumer electronic stores. They are small, compact, and usually weigh less than a few pounds. Since the entire camera will fit into the palm of your hand, they are occasionally referred to as palmcorders. These cameras offer the lowest picture quality of the three categories, but they are still capable of producing video images that are better than some of the full-sized cameras of the early 1990s. These cameras are available in both one-chip and three-chip configurations. Common recording formats for this category are miniDV, Digital8, and DVD discs. The cost of these cameras can run from $300 to $1,500.

Prosumer

Mid-sized "prosumer" cameras fall between the previous two categories. They weigh between two and 11 pounds and may support miniDV, DVCAM, DVCPRO, DV, or HDV recording formats. These cameras are also available with one-chip or three-chip technology. They usually produce a picture quality that is better than consumer cameras but not quite as good as the better professional models. The cost of these cameras can run from $1,500 to $5,000.

Recording Formats

Most of the media formats being used today for videotaping are digital. This means that the video information the camera receives is recorded onto tape (or disc or another format) using a method similar to that of computers or compact discs. As you may have noticed from the previous paragraphs, there are several to choose from. Here are the ones you need to be aware of.

Digital8

This is one of the formats used in Sony's consumer cameras and will record up to one hour per tape. Digital8 cameras will play the analog videotape formats that came before it, 8mm and Hi8. This format is expected to be discontinued soon.

MiniDV

Currently, this is the most popular format being used in consumer and pro-sumer cameras. These tapes will hold up to 60 and even 80 minutes of video when you record in SP mode and up to 120 minutes in LP. Almost every brand of camcorder offers a miniDV-compatible camera.

DV

DV is similar to miniDV in how it records onto the tape, but DV tapes are physically larger than miniDV tapes and can hold more video.

DVCAM

This format is found exclusively on Sony professional camcorders and can hold up to 184 minutes of video. It is very popular with wedding and event videographers who prefer to use the professional full-sized cameras. The recording speed of this format is 33 percent faster than miniDV, allowing the video information to be spread out over larger sections of tape. It is supposed to have fewer dropout problems than miniDV. It is also larger in size than the miniDV tape.

> **VIDEO TERM** SP refers to the standard play recording mode on camcorders, which provides the best quality for recording. LP refers to the long play or extended play recording mode on camcorders. This feature is more likely to be found on consumer models than professional cameras. It advances the videotape more slowly than the SP mode does. This tradeoff sacrifices a little picture quality in exchange for getting more video on a tape.

DVCPRO

DVCPRO is Panasonic's equivalent to DVCAM and holds up to 126 minutes of video. It is also larger in size than the miniDV tape.

DVD

There are currently some consumer camcorders on the market that will record on small DVD discs. This has not been proven to be a good fit for the wedding video industry at this time.

Betacam (and Betacam SP)

Betacam is primarily used by television stations, networks, and big-budget production companies for producing broadcast-quality programs. Even though many programs (or portions of programs) have been shot on miniDV, Betacam is still considered a standard format for broadcasters such as television stations and networks. This is considered an analog media and can record up to 90 minutes on a tape.

Digital Betacam

Digital Betacam (also called "Digi-Beta") is similar to Betacam but records digitally rather than analog.

HDV or HDCAM

These are two of the newest formats that have come onto the market. They're intended to capture images at high-definition quality. Although there are many editing systems that will edit in this format, there isn't currently a media format available that can record high-definition video and will play on a client's video player. And, as of this writing, none of my clients have been asking for this quality of video. This could change over the next three to five years, but for now I don't feel it's worth pursuing for the arena of wedding video.

Formats Used Most by Wedding Videographers

The three most commonly used formats in the wedding video industry are miniDV, DVCAM, and DVCPRO, with miniDV being the most popular and DVCPRO being the least used by wedding videographers. I don't know many professionals who can really tell the difference in the quality of any of these three formats. Usually, videographers will choose a camera based on the characteristics, performance, and price of the camera and not on the type of tape they use.

Chip Size

All of the new camcorders being sold today use CCDs (charge-coupled devices, a type of computer chip) to convert the visual information gathered by the camera's lens into electrical impulses that can be recorded onto a videotape. The size of the chip determines how much detail the camera will be able to capture; the larger the chip, the better the quality of the picture. Cameras containing larger chips are usually more expensive and produce a better picture quality.

Single-Chip vs. Three-Chip Cameras

If you were to look at the surface of the screen on your television set with a magnifying glass and the TV turned on, you would notice that the picture is made up of many rows of little squares or dots (referred to as pixels), in three different colors—red, green, and blue. The old front-projected, large-screen televisions used to have three separate projection lamps, one for each of these colors. The various combinations of these three colors make up the color images you see on your color TV.

VIDEO TERM CCD stands for Charge Coupled Device. For a further explanation on this go to: http://huizen.ddsw.nl/bewoners/maan/imaging/camera/camera.html

Camcorders will often be referred to as having a single chip (one-chip) or three chips. Three-chip cameras use three CCDs instead of one. Each CCD is responsible for handling each of the primary colors associated with television picture reproduction. Three-chip cameras generally produce a better picture quality than a single chip. For this reason, most professional wedding videographers prefer to use the three-chip cameras. When it comes to the quality of the wedding video, three-chip cameras help separate the professional from family members offering to tape the event for free. We'll talk more about this topic later.

Additional Camera Features

Most of the professional and prosumer camcorders come with additional features that will become extremely beneficial to your productions. In this section, we'll cover some of these features.

As with photo cameras, it's a welcome benefit when your video camera allows you to control various settings for the images you're capturing. Some of these settings are iris, shutter speed, focus, and white balance. We'll discuss these in more detail in Chapter 4. I strongly encourage you to consider purchasing a camera with the ability to manually adjust all of these features.

Interchangeable Lenses

Some camcorders allow you to remove the lens and attach different types of lenses, such as wide-angle, zoom, and fish-eye lenses. Most of these cameras are sold with zoom lenses that allow you to zoom in on the subject for a close-up or zoom out for a wide-angle shot. The most important benefit of cameras with interchangeable lenses is that you'll have the ability to use a higher-quality lens than the cameras that use a built-in lens.

Audio Inputs

Most of the camcorders you should be considering will come with an external microphone input or inputs that will allow you to use a different microphone than the one built into or attached to the camera. I strongly encourage you to select a camcorder with this option.

Volume Controls

Most prosumer and professional camcorders come with volume controls that allow you to adjust the level of the audio coming into the camera. This is another feature that is highly recommended.

Flip-Out View Screens

Many camcorders are now coming with an LCD video screen attached to the side of the camera that flips outward so that you can monitor what the lens is capturing without having to look through the viewfinder. See Figure 2-1. This is a nice feature, but it's not mandatory; if the camera comes with it that's fine.

Video Light Connector

Some of the more expensive prosumer and professional, full-sized cameras come with a video light connector. This feature is nice because it allows you to

Figure 2-1
Flip-out screen.

connect a video light directly into the camcorder and operate the light using the camera's power supply. This eliminates the need for you to wear a heavy battery belt around your waist. Many of these cameras will also turn the light on automatically when you push the record button and turn the light off when you push the button again, returning the camera to pause mode. This is a very nice benefit. It is also helpful in that when the light is on you'll know you are recording.

Brands

The most common brands of cameras you'll find being used for weddings are Sony, Panasonic, JVC, and Canon.

Congratulations! You made it through some of the toughest information on the subject of cameras. You may want to read the previous material again until you become comfortable with it. Now, we can go on to what it all means.

How to Choose a Camera

To summarize what we've covered so far, a two-thirds-inch three-CCD professional camera will almost always outperform a single CCD consumer camera, but at a cost. A consumer camera containing a single CCD would probably sell for around $400. The professional camera with the three two-thirds-inch CCDs would most likely sell for around $10,000 to $15,000. As you can see, that's quite a difference.

Recommendations

So, how do you determine which camera you should buy? Let's start with the features you *must* have on the camera. You should definitely look for a camera with:

·   Manual iris, shutter speed, focus, and white balance controls
·   Manual audio level controls
·   External microphone input or inputs

I recommend a camera in the prosumer or professional categories with three CCDs. Cameras that record on DV, DVCAM, DVCPRO, or miniDV are sufficient. The rest of the decision will be up to you based on how much money you're comfortable investing, how nice you want your picture quality to be, and what level of clientele that you'll ultimately want to attract. We'll cover more on clientele levels in Chapter 6.

For the last five years or so, I have been using a professional, full-sized, two-thirds inch three chip camera and have been very pleased with the results. However, when I first started in the wedding video business, I didn't have the $10,000 to invest in such a camera. So, I started with a prosumer, one-third-inch, three-chip camera I picked up for around $3,000. If you ever want to be taken seriously as a professional by your clients, I would never recommend using the $400 cameras. The features and performance of the prosumer cameras will be well worth the difference in price over the long term.

Tripods

Once you've picked out your camcorder, you'll need to get a good tripod to go with it. Professional tripods cost quite a bit more than the ones sold at most consumer electronic stores, ranging from $250 to over $3,000. You'll pay more for tripods that have more features and operate more smoothly.

Fluid-Head

You'll definitely want to get a fluid-head tripod. Fluid-head tripods allow you to pan your camera from side to side and up and down in a continuously smooth motion. This becomes really important when you're in a situation when you have to zoom the camera all of the way in and follow a moving subject. More on this in Chapter 4.

Ball Level

Some tripods come with something called a ball level for the head. This feature allows you to quickly level your camera without having to adjust the length of any of the tripod's legs. It's a nice feature but not mandatory if you're trying to save some money.

Other Considerations

A carrying case for the tripod is nice but not mandatory. There are several different models of tripods available from each manufacturer. Each is designed with a different purpose in mind. You should be concerned mainly with whether the tripod is built to handle the weight of your camera. A knowledgable salesperson should be able to help you choose the right tripod to accommodate the weight of your camera.

Brands

The most common brands of tripods you'll find are Bogen/Manfrotto, Sachtler, Vinten, Miller, Cartoni, and Gitzo. The Bogen/Manfrotto tripods tend to be lower-priced than the others. I suggest looking at the different tripods in person to see if you like how they "feel" and operate when you use them.

Tripod Dollies

Many tripod manufacturers make dollies that can attach to the legs of their tripods. The dolly provides the ability to roll or move the tripod and camera around smoothly when necessary. It is more difficult to move the tripod smoothly with the camera mounted on top of it. The tripod dolly will enable you to perform "dolly shots" with your camera. I've used the dolly to move the camera around in a church. You don't need one right away, but it's something to consider. I'll go over one possible use for it in Chapter 10.

Battery Belts

Battery belts consist of several battery cells that are mounted onto a belt strap that attaches around your waist. The battery cells are rechargeable, and the belt usually comes with a charger. Most battery belts can power a camera for several hours or camera lights for a few hours. The larger (and heavier) battery cells will power a camera and lights for longer periods of time. Most of the newer cameras will operate for longer periods of time on the newer extended-length batteries that attach directly to the camera. This decreases the need for a battery belt to power the camera.

MOVIE TERM The term "dolly shot" originated in the film industry and refers to the process of moving the camera towards or away from the subject you are filming.

Lights

You'll definitely want to get a light for your camera. When it's time to shoot a wedding reception in a dark location, you'll need to have a light on your camera. If you purchased a camera that has the video light connector (mentioned earlier), then you'll probably want to choose a light from Anton Bauer or Frezzi. Both of these companies offer lights that attach to the top of the camera and plug into the camera's power outlet (usually located near the mounting location of the light). Otherwise, there are several choices for lighting.

Powering the Light

There are some lights that will run on a rechargeable battery that attaches to the back of the light. Sony makes one like this. Other lights will most likely require a battery belt for power.

Wattage

Most of the newer cameras on the market are designed to operate fairly well in low light, such as at a wedding reception. But you will still want to use a light in order to maintain a nice picture quality. You should be able to get by with a light that is 30 watts or less.

Brands

The most common brands of lights are Anton Bauer, Frezzi, NRG, Cool Lux, Arri, Sony, and Bescor. If you're planning on powering the light from a battery belt, NRG and Frezzi make a nice light with a built-in dimmer.

Microphones

Audio accounts for 50 percent of the production value of a video. It is *just* as important as the picture. In fact, in my experience, clients are more likely to notice problems in the sound than in the picture. Therefore, I recommend that you not cut corners in this area.

Types of Microphones

There's a lot to know about microphones; I've conducted half-day seminars on this topic alone. I'm going to stay with the basics that apply to weddings. There are wireless and wired microphones. Lavaliere, handheld, camera, and shotgun mics are the main types used for weddings.

Wireless vs. Wired

Most sound engineers will tell you that wired mics are preferred over wireless. There's a good reason for this. Wireless mics are exposed to the possibility of radio waves interfering with the sound, whereas wired mics are much less susceptible to this. However, in the case of weddings, wireless mics are much more practical to use. This will be discussed in more detail in Chapter 9.

Wired mics, as the name implies, requires attaching one end of a mic cable to the microphone and the other into the camera or an audio mixer. Therefore, the mic can never be farther away from the camera (or mixer) than the length of the cable. The mic cable may pose the danger of tripping people who walk around the area where the cable has been placed.

I've used nothing but wireless microphones throughout my wedding video career. For example, I'll clip a wireless mic on the groom's tuxedo so, that when he walks around the church I won't have to worry about him or anyone else tripping over a mic cable. The most common type of wireless mic used in weddings is a lavaliere (or lav) mic, a small microphone that can be clipped onto the groom's lapel. Attached to the mic is a small wire that connects it to a transmitter that is clipped onto the groom's belt or the waistband of his pants. I usually hide this wire underneath the tuxedo jacket. The transmitter is about the size of a deck of cards and is nicely concealed by the groom's jacket. The receiver is located near my audio mixer, which is then fed into the camera so that I will be able to record the bride and groom's vows clearly.

UHF vs. VHF

Cell phones, radio, television, and police radios are just a few of the modern communication systems that use radio waves to transmit and receive information through the air without the use of cables. If you could see a radio wave it might resemble a ripple created by throwing a pebble into a calm pond. Radio waves can be different lengths. Each of these different lengths represents a radio frequency. Each type of communication system uses a range of frequencies. Occasionally, two different communication devices are transmitting on the same or nearly the same frequency, which causes what we call interference. If this happens with our wireless mic, our equipment will record undesirable noise that may keep us from understanding the words being picked up by the mic.

There are two main radio frequency ranges for wireless microphones. They are referred to as UHF and VHF. Unfortunately, television stations are still broadcasting their signals in both of these ranges. Fortunately, they are not using all of the frequencies within those ranges. Now, you see why there may be a potential threat of interference when we use wireless mics.

Most videographers have chosen to use wireless mics in the UHF range, as UHF mics are capable of transmitting longer distances without as much potential interference as VHF mics. UHF mics have proven to be more reliable.

Frequencies Within UHF

The UHF range contains thousands of different frequencies. Most UHF wireless mic systems come with the ability to choose from among 100 or more frequencies. The benefit here is that if you happen to be working in a geographic region where you're getting interference with your wireless mic, you can change the frequency to eliminate the interference. This is sort of like driving down a multilane highway and changing lanes when a vehicle or object is blocking your lane.

Diversity and True-Diversity Systems

Wireless mic systems also come in "diversity" and "true-diversity" configurations. An inexpensive wireless mic may have a receiver that has only one antenna to receive the signal from the transmitter. A diversity system has two antennas so that at any given time one antenna may be better positioned to receive the signal than the other one. Even though this system has two antennas, it uses only one receiver for both. A true-diversity mic system has two separate receivers (one dedicated for each antenna) for receiving the signal. The premise is that two receivers are better than one and should function better.

Microphone Pickup Patterns

There are several different types of audio pickup patterns that differentiate various microphones from each other. There is a video that covers the topic of pickup patterns, including illustrations, available at www.provideotraining.com. For wedding videos, you'll mainly be using lavaliere mics that have an omnidirectional pickup pattern. Most wireless mic systems are sold with this type of mic.

Lavaliere Mics

As mentioned earlier in the section on wired vs. wireless, the lavaliere, or lav mic, is a small mic clipped onto the lapel of the groom's tuxedo that plugs into the transmitter attached to the groom's belt. It is used to record vows from the bride and groom. It is also used for other aspects of the wedding ceremony, which will be covered later in Chapter 9.

Handheld Mics

Just as it sounds, the handheld mic gets its name from the fact that you usually hold it in your hand while you speak or sing into it. The most common use for the handheld mic is for recording messages from guests during the wedding reception. Some videographers will use a cable to connect this mic to their camera. I prefer to use a plug-on transmitter with the handheld mic. This is another type of wireless mic system where the transmitter plugs onto the end of the handheld mic, in place of a cable, which allows the sound captured from this mic to be transmitted to the receiver on the camera without any wires. This allows me to be further away from the person holding the mic. For example, it helps when I interview a large group of people and need to get them all in the shot. It also means you don't have to worry about cables getting in the way and being tripped over.

NOTE: Handheld mics are sometimes referred to as "stick mics" since they are shaped much like a stick or baton.

Camera Mic

The camera mic is the microphone that comes with the camera, either built into the camera or attached to the camera. It is normally used for capturing the ambient sound of the event that you are videotaping. Ambient sound refers to all of the sounds you would be hearing if you are at the event. When you're videotaping in a church, you would hear people's voices with the echoes from the church's acoustics mixed in. The camera's mic would hear it the same way.

Shotgun Mics

Shotgun mics get their name from the way they look. They look like the barrel of a shotgun. They are used mainly for when you need to record sound from one specific location or direction. I haven't needed to use a shotgun mic for any of the weddings I've taped, but it's good to be aware of them.

Brands

The most common brands of mics you'll hear about are Audio-Technica, Azden, Lectrosonics, Samson, Sennheiser, Shure, Sony, and Telex. Each brand tends to use a different set of frequencies.

Recommendations

I recommend using UHF true-diversity wireless lav mic systems. They cost from $400 and up. I also recommend getting a system with a plug-on transmitter, and don't forget to buy a handheld mic to go with it. You can find good handheld mics for under $100.

If you're planning on purchasing two or more systems, I suggest choosing two different brands of mics. The reason for this is that if you experience interference with one of your mic systems that you can't seem to get rid of, you could switch to the other brand. This should solve your interference problem quickly, most of the time. Also, there have been some locations that I've worked in where one brand just would not work very well. When I switched to the other brand, I had no more problems.

When you reach a point that you're planning on having three or more systems, then you may consider buying a second system of the same brand and model as one of your other systems.

Accessories for Shooting

Before you go out on a shoot, you need to make sure you have some essential cables, adapters, and accessories in your accessory bag. The first thing to get is a bag to carry these items in. I find a duffle bag with several pockets to be quite useful. Camera stores sell cases that look like carry-on luggage, but when you open them, there are several dividers attached with Velcro that divide the interior into several small compartments that you can put things into.

Batteries

This should be obvious, but let's go over all of the different types of batteries you should keep on hand. The most important batteries to have on hand are the batteries and backup batteries required to operate your camcorder. I suggest taking your camera out somewhere with fully charged batteries. Videotape anything until the battery is drained. Make a note as to how long it lasted. With this information, you should be able to determine how many batteries to get. The minimum I recommend to have is at least three batteries (fully charged) for your camera. And *always* take the charger and AC adapter with you.

The wireless microphones you have selected will require either 9-volt or AA batteries. I always take at least 10 of each on shoots. If you will be using a battery belt to power your light, always make sure it is fully charged before each shoot. I suggest getting a second battery belt, as wedding receptions can run long and lights tend to drain batteries fairly quickly. If you're going to use the lights with the battery pack that attaches to the back, you should have a few extra batteries for that also. You should have extra batteries for anything else you plan to use on your shoots.

Power and Extension Cables

Always be sure to take your camera's power (AC) cable and any other power cables that your other equipment might operate on. This always makes for a good backup in case something happens to your batteries. Take some long extension cables for power in case you do have to plug your camera into an AC outlet. You can pick these up at your local hardware store or a Home Depot. Twenty-five foot, 50-foot, and even 100-foot cables may come in handy sometime.

Microphone Cables

In addition to having a handheld mic, you will need a cable to connect the mic to your camera. This mic may be used for recording interviews or messages from guests. For this reason, make sure you have a long enough cable; 15 to 25 feet should do. This becomes a backup mic if your wireless mic system fails or if you haven't purchased one yet.

Adapters

Be sure to have all necessary adapters for connecting all of your equipment in your bag.

Tapes

Most videographers experience fewer problems with their digital tapes when they stay with the same brand. I use the brand of tape that is made by the same company that makes my camera. And I always take along a few extra blank videotapes on my shoots. You never know when a tape is defective or whether you'll run out of tape before the event is over.

Dolly or Cart

One of the best investments I ever made was buying a fold-up, two-wheel dolly for carrying camera and equipment cases. It's been a real back-saver, since carrying a lot of heavy equipment around can be real hard on your back. Some videographers use a cart instead.

Backup Equipment

In order to be considered a *true professional*, you need to have backup equipment in case any piece of equipment should fail to function. This means having replacement light bulbs for your light, extra batteries, extra tapes, an extra mic—both handheld and wireless and if possible an extra camera. I know that might sound expensive, but it could be more expensive trying to explain to the bride why you didn't get any footage of her wedding. I've heard that in some states a bride could sue her DJ for ruining the wedding for an amount up to the *entire* cost of the wedding. Ouch.

If you can't afford to buy backups for everything right away, start with the most important ones first. Also, it doesn't hurt to have an after-hours contact phone number for another videographer or an equipment rental company that could rent you the necessary equipment in case yours fails. At one of the weddings I shot, we were contracted to provide the video projector for showing a montage at the reception. When it came time to set up the unit and get it ready for use, we discovered that the motorized focus control had seized up and there was no way to manually focus the projector. After trying for about 30 minutes, I couldn't get it to work. I only owned one projector so I didn't have a backup. I was forced to rent one from the hotel we were shooting in and I had to pay for it out of my own pocket. They charged me $450! I had charged my client only about $250, so I had to absorb the difference. I can't stress enough the importance of having backup equipment.

Equipment for Editing

Linear vs. Nonlinear Editing Systems

There are two types of editing methods that you'll need to know about: linear and nonlinear.

Linear

Linear refers to how you perform your edits. Usually, linear editing is done by selecting a video clip and copying it from one VCR to another VCR. Then you select another video clip and copy it, and so on. On the tape you are recording to, you are adding the various video clips one at a time until you reach the end of your program or the end of the tape, whichever occurs first.

Nonlinear

Nonlinear editing is typically performed using software, which is often referred to as a nonlinear editor due to how the edits are performed. The editor selects various clips from the raw footage and capture (or record) them into the computer. Once all of the necessary clips have been captured, the editor will then assemble them on a timeline. The clips can be placed on the timeline in any order, regardless of where they physically exist on the computer's hard drive, therefore, the term "nonlinear." The convenience of this process make it the preferred choice of most editors. The only downside is that this process usually takes longer to edit than the linear method. The nonlinear method does allow for more creativity in the editing process.

Nonlinear Editing Computer and Software

The current prices of nonlinear editing systems have become so low that there is no reason to consider using a linear system. There are several brands of nonlinear editors on the market, including Avid, Apple Final Cut Pro, Adobe Premiere, Vegas, and more. If you prefer using Apple computers, then Final Cut Pro will be the editing software you'll want to use. If you prefer PCs, then you'll have a few more choices of editing software.

The movie industry and industrial video production houses are the largest users of the Avid editing system. The Avid systems can easily run up to $100,000. This is why most wedding videographers don't use this system. Apple's Final Cut Pro has become the movie industry's second-favorite choice and has been gaining a lot of popularity in the wedding and event industry. Adobe Premiere and Vegas offer a substantially lower-priced alternative for PC users.

When shopping for computers, faster CPUs (processors) are preferred. Since this is the main control unit for everything the computer does, it needs to be fast. You should try to get a system that uses one hard drive for the software and a separate hard drive for the video clips. The editing systems tend to run better this way. I recommend at least 40GB for the system drive (that will contain your software programs) and at least 120GB for the video drive. Video tends to use a lot of hard drive space in a hurry. You should have a minimum of 1GB of RAM memory. Your computer will need some way to capture the video either via a FireWire cable or through a video capture card. I also recommend getting a large monitor, at least 19 inches. Many videographers have decided to use two monitors for the editing. This allows them to spread the editing program display over a larger viewing area. Computer technology changes so fast that I can't really make any specific recommendations as to what equipment to buy.

Other Software to Consider

I strongly encourage getting a copy of Adobe Photoshop. I use Photoshop almost as much as my editing program. It won't be long before you will get a client who will want to put photos in their video, and Photoshop is a great program for working with photos. A program for copying music from CDs (often referred to as a CD ripper) may also come in handy.

Scanner

If you're going to be working with photos, you should have a scanner as well for scanning the photos into your computer.

DVD Burner

A DVD burner records video information onto a DVD. There are two ways to create DVDs: using a DVD burner in a computer or using a standalone burner. A standalone burner is a separate unit, similar to a VCR that will record video from another source such as a VCR, camcorder, or computer in "real time" (the actual length of the program). The standalone burner is connected to the source via FireWire or traditional analog audio and video cables. The recording process is similar to recording with a standard VHS VCR. I refer to DVDs created this way as "unauthored" DVDs since they do not require the use of an authoring program.

DVD burners in computers are set up a little differently. The video needs to be encoded into a special file format, MPEG-2 (discussed in Chapter 4), and a menu needs to be created before the information can be burned onto a disc. I refer to DVDs created this way as "authored" DVDs since they do require an authoring program. There are several authoring programs on the market. Some of the current programs available are Ulead's DVD Workshop, Adobe Encore, DVDit, and DVD Architect.

Standalone burners run around a few hundred dollars. You may be able to find computer DVD burners for under $100. I've used both types in my studio, and I recommend the computer-based burner because you can create professional-looking discs that will enable you to charge more money for your services. The process involved in using these two methods will be covered in more detail later in Chapter 4.

Video Recorders

Regardless of which method you choose, linear or nonlinear, you'll need to get at least one video recorder (VCR). I recommend a recorder that uses the same videotape format as the one you've chosen for the camcorder. For example, if you decided to purchase a miniDV camera, make sure you buy a deck that will play and record on miniDV. If you decide to use a nonlinear editing system, then you should be able to get by with one deck. A linear system will require at least two decks. Since most of the video equipment being used by professional videographers today is digital, you'll probably want to make sure the deck has FireWire or the capability to link to digital devices.

Video Monitors

You'll need to get at least one video monitor for your editing station. Many videographers have been using a 13-inch or 20-inch television set to monitor the video from their editing system or VCR. If you're able to invest more for your video monitor, I suggest getting a production monitor (see Figure 2–2).

They provide a more accurate representation of what your video really looks like than a typical television set provides.

Figure 2–2
Production monitor.

How Much Should You Expect to Invest in Equipment?

You can expect to invest between $10,000 and $15,000 for an entry-level setup. A high-quality, truly professional package will start at $20,000. Before you rush out to buy your equipment, make sure you've put aside at least $5,000 for marketing to get your business up and running. I've watched too many video companies fail and go out of business because they invested too much money into equipment and not enough into marketing. This will be addressed in more detail in Chapter 6.

Buying vs. Leasing

People have different opinions on which method is better, buying or leasing equipment. The benefit of buying your equipment is that you will own it. It's yours to do whatever you please with. You can even sell it later if you like. The disadvantage is that you have to come up with the full purchase price at the time of purchase. If you choose to finance your equipment purchase, then you'll have payments spread out over two to five years depending on the arrangements you've made with the finance company. You will pay interest on this loan but the interest is tax-deductible. Consult your tax advisor regarding deductibility of your equipment purchases.

The benefit of leasing is that you will make payments instead of coming up with the full purchase price and the payments are usually less than if you took out a loan. The disadvantage is that you don't own the equipment, and therefore you won't establish any equity in the equipment and you can't sell it later. The entire lease payments are typically tax-deductible, though. Again, you should consult your tax advisor regarding deductibility of your equipment leasing. There are some lease programs with a low "buy-out" option. This means at the end of the lease term, the leasing company will let you buy the equipment for a small additional charge.

Everyone's financial situation is different, so it will be up to you as to which option is better for your business.

Where to Buy Equipment

There are many choices for purchasing your equipment. Check your local yellow pages under Video Equipment—Sales for local places that may sell the equipment you're looking for. Every April the National Association of Broadcasters (NAB) holds its convention and trade show in Las Vegas. Thousands of different kinds of video, audio, and related equipment are on display from various manufacturers. Sometimes you can get some great deals at the trade show. Go to your local videographer association's next meeting and ask some of the members where they buy their gear.

There are other companies selling video gear that can be located on the Internet. Here are just a few of them:

B&H Photo & Video	www.bhphotovideo.com
Armatos	www.armatosvideo.com
ProMax	www.promax.com

Summary

There is a lot of different equipment on the market. Start your business with a good three-chip professional or prosumer camera with manual iris, shutter, focus, and white balance controls and an external microphone input. Use a sturdy, fluid-head tripod. Make sure you have at least one wireless microphone system and a handheld mic with a cable. Don't forget about the camera light, extra camera batteries, and plenty of 9-volt and AA batteries based on your equipment.

I recommend a nonlinear computer editing system with a DVD burner, along with a VCR, computer monitor, and a video monitor. And don't forget to budget some money for marketing.

Hopefully, this chapter has provided you with enough information to make good decisions on what to buy. Periodically throughout the year, there are intensive courses offered on how to choose the right gear for you. These courses cover the various types and brands of equipment out there and the pros and cons of each of them. If you'd like more information on these courses, you can call ProVideo Training at 877-362-0741 or visit www.provideotraining.com. They're very comprehensive seminars.

Chapter 3
Setting Up Your Equipment

Before we get started on hooking up your equipment, we need to go over the different types of cables, connectors, and adapters that you need to be familiar with. Many of them you will be using.

Cables and Connectors

As you venture further into your new career, you'll need to become very familiar with what these items look like, what they're called, and when to use them.

Video Cables and Connectors

There are five types of video cables: BNC, S-Video, RCA, coaxial, and component.

BNC

The BNC cable (see Figure 3-1) is commonly used with the more expensive professional equipment. Sometimes it is referred to as composite. It's not important to know what composite means; just be aware of the term.

Figure 3-1
BNC cable.

RCA

RCA video cable (see Figure 3-2) is the most basic connection for video. It is usually color-coded yellow for video. It is sometimes referred to as phono or composite video cable.

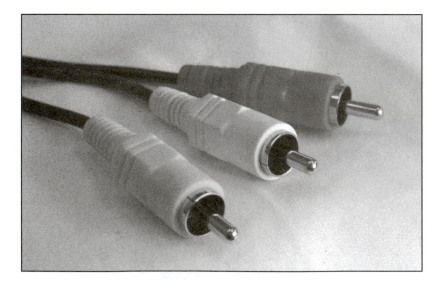

Figure 3-2
RCA video cable.

S-Video

The S-Video cable (see Figure 3-3) has four pins inside the collar on both ends. These pins are arranged in a trapezoidal pattern. S-Video cables divide the video signal into two parts: the color (sometimes referred to as chrominance) and the brightness (sometimes referred to as luminance). If you're using these cables and you happen to notice that the picture portion of your video seems to have lost its color, check the pins at both ends. One of them may be bent or broken. S-Video cables provide better picture quality than RCA video cables.

Figure 3-3
S-Video cable.

Coaxial

Coaxial (or coax) cable (see Figure 3-4) is most commonly used for hooking up cable TV, satellite, or VCRs to television sets.

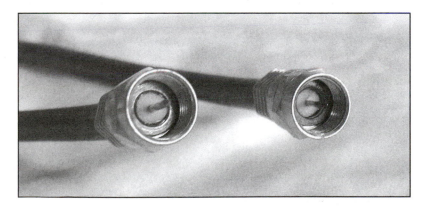

Figure 3-4
Coaxial cable.

Component

Component cables (see Figure 3-5) may have three RCA- or three BNC-style connectors on the ends of the cable. The BNC version has been used for high-end professional equipment. The RCA version is now being used for hooking up DVD players and high-definition television tuner boxes. Each of the three cables carries the respective information for the red, green, and blue parts of the signal. (Refer to the three-chip description of cameras in the previous chapter.) This cable delivers the highest picture quality from an analog source.

Figure 3-5
Component cable.

Audio Cables and Connectors

There are four common types of audio cables: RCA, XLR, 1/4-inch, and 1/8-inch miniplug.

RCA

RCA cables (see Figure 3-6) are the most basic connection for audio. They are usually color-coded red and black or red and white. The red typically is used for right channel audio of a stereo signal and black (or white) for the left channel of audio. Often the jacks on the back of the equipment will have colors to match these. RCA cables are sometimes referred to as phono cables.

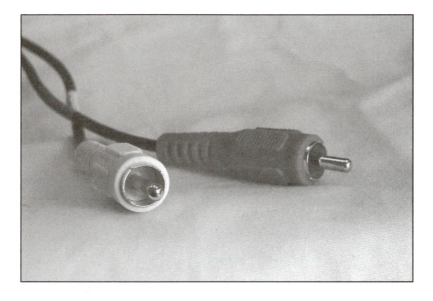

Figure 3-6
BNC cable.

XLR

The XLR cable (see Figure 3-7) is considered the professional choice for the transfer of audio signals. The primary reason is due to the shielding it has for rejecting radio frequency interference (RFI) which then reduces the amount of noise in the sound, particularly when you have to run the cables over a long distance.

Figure 3-7
XLR cable.

Quarter-inch or headphone

The quarter-inch (see Figure 3-8) is occasionally used in video but is not as common as XLR. They are sometimes referred to as headphone plugs since years ago most headphones used this plug to connect into stereo systems.

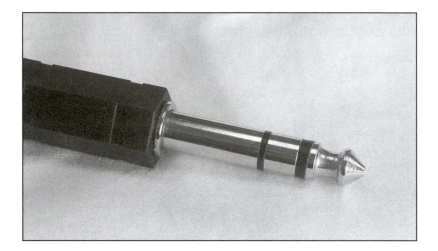

Figure 3-8
Quarter-inch cable.

1/8-inch or miniplug

The miniplug (see Figure 3-9) cables are more common for microphone inputs on the smaller prosumer or consumer camcorders.

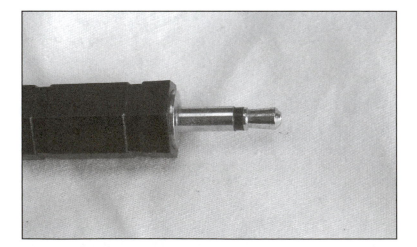

Figure 3-9
Miniplug cable.

Setting Up Editing Equipment

Now that you're familiar with some of the cable types, it's time to hook up your editing system. Since most of today's videographers are using computerized editors, I'm going to assume you've purchased a computer for nonlinear editing.

Nonlinear Computer System

Follow the setup instructions you received with your computer for hooking up the keyboard, mouse, monitor, and other devices. Your computer should have come with either a FireWire jack or a video capture card (with or without a breakout box).

FireWire Connection

If your computer has only a FireWire connection (Figure 3-10), then you will plug one end of a FireWire cable into the computer and the other end into your digital VCR. Consult your editing software manual on how to capture video into your computer. The FireWire cable is sometimes referred to as an IEEE 1394 cable.

BREAKOUT BOX: A breakout box usually refers to a separate panel of jacks for hooking your audio and video cables to. This may be attached to the front of the computer (where your DVD drive is), or it may be a separate piece that will sit on top of your desk.

Figure 3-10
FireWire cable.

Figure 3-11
Break-out box.

Video Capture Card

If your video capture card has a breakout box (see Figure 3-11), then you should be able to use the RCA or XLR connections to hook the audio from your digital VCR into your computer. The video will hook up using one of the video connectors previously described. If your video capture card does not have a breakout box, then it may have RCA jacks for the audio and either an S-Video or RCA jack for the video. Most likely this card will be located on the back of the computer, and that's where you'll plug in these cables. You may need to consult the dealer where you purchased the computer regarding these connections. The other end of the cables should plug into your digital VCR. If not, you'll need to get some adapters to convert the cable connectors to fit the jacks on your VCR.

You will need to hook up two sets of cables. One will go from the audio and video outputs (often labeled Play) on the VCR to the inputs on your computer, and the other will go from the audio and video inputs (often labeled Record) on the VCR to the outputs on your computer. You should consult your video editing software manual on how to capture video into your computer.

The Video Monitor

The video monitor can be hooked up to your digital VCR using the second set of outputs on the digital VCR.

Production Monitor

If you've decided to use a production monitor, the RCA audio outputs from your deck may have to be connected to a Y-adapter before being connected to the monitor as the monitor may only have one audio input. The video can be connected using either an S-Video or BNC cable. Check the back of both the monitor and the VCR to be sure which type you'll need.

Consumer Monitor

If you've decided to use a consumer monitor (your regular television set), then you'll be using RCA cables for the audio and maybe the video as well. If your monitor has an S-Video input, I recommend using that instead for the video. Check the back of both the monitor and the VCR to be sure which type you'll need.

Audio Mixer (Optional)

In my editing system, I use a Mackie audio mixer (see Figure 3-12). I have each channel of audio (left and right) plugged into the audio mixer using two separate inputs. Each input has its own volume knob so that I can adjust the level of each independent of the other. This setup allows me to mix both channels of audio and then send the final mix out to both channels of audio for the video. I'll talk more about why you might want to do this in the next section. You don't have to have an audio mixer in your editing system.

Setting Up Camera and Mics for Videotaping

I strongly encourage you to practice setting up your camera and microphone equipment many times before you ever go out on a paid shoot. You'll want to know your equipment inside and out.

Figure 3-12
Audio mixer

Camera

For many of your shoots, you'll be using a tripod. If you're not using a tripod, skip to the next step. To set up the tripod simply extend all three of the legs to the height you prefer. Try to make sure they are all even. Also make sure they are all tightened down so the tripod won't fall over when the camera is put on top. If your tripod has a ball level, this is the time to adjust it so that it is level. There are two common types of camera mounts for the tripod. One is a hexagonal-shaped mount that screws into the bottom of the camera and then drops into position on top of the tripod and has a lever to secure the locking mechanism into place. The other is a slide plate that screws into the bottom of the camera and then slides onto the tripod. Once you have slid the plate into the tripod's groove, there should be a lever on the side that will lock the plate into place so it won't slide back and forth. Now that your camera is secure on the tripod you're ready for the next step.

Attaching the Battery or AC adapter

Now attach the battery or plug in the AC adapter to power the camera. If you haven't done so already, put a blank tape into the camera.

Hooking Up Microphones

Depending on the type of camera you've purchased, you'll either have an XLR or a miniplug jack for hooking up external microphones. For cameras with XLR jacks (see Figure 3-13), there are usually two of them; one is labeled channel 1, the other is channel 2. Your mic should have an XLR output. You can plug it into either of these two channels. If you're only using one mic then your camera's built-in mic should feed sound to the other channel. If you're going to use two mics, plug each one into each of the two channels. Be aware that using two mics will not allow you to use the camera's built-in mic for ambient sound. Using headphones, make sure both channels are receiving sound.

If your camera has a miniplug jack for an external mic (see Figure 3-14) then you will only have one input, although it should be a stereo input. Be aware that when you plug any cable into this jack, you will automatically by-

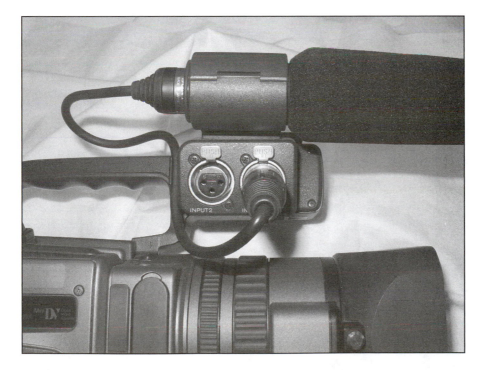

Figure 3-13
XLR jack

Figure 3-14
Mini-plug jack.

pass the camera's built-in mic. You can use only one mic. Make sure your mic has a miniplug connector. In order to hook up more than one mic, you will need either an audio mixer (similar to what I described earlier) or a special adapter. Whenever possible, I recommend attaching a short shotgun or hand-held mic to the camera and connecting it to a second channel using one of the mixers described in the next section. This will become your new ambient mic since you've bypassed the camera's mic.

Audio Mixers

Azden makes a pager-sized audio mixer (model CAM 3) that allows you to plug in three miniplug mics, and it has one stereo miniplug cable to connect to your camera. This allows you to adjust the volume levels for all three mics independently. The audio from the first mic will be sent to the left channel of the camera's audio, the audio from the second mic will be sent to the right channel, and the audio from the third mic will be sent to both channels.

Beachtek makes an adapter that allows you to hook up two XLR mics. There is a stereo miniplug that plugs into the camera. Each XLR input has a separate volume control knob to adjust the mic level going into each channel.

Mackie makes several professional mixers that will allow you to hook up multiple microphones and send the output into either one or two channels. This mixer, with the use of the right adapters, can be used with either camera type.

There are detailed training videos and seminars that cover everything you might want to know about all of the different audio hookup possibilities and how to perform them on ProVideo's website at www.provideotraining.com.

Recording Two Channels of Audio

Whenever possible, I suggest recording two channels of audio—the camera's mic or a separate camera-mounted mic to record ambient audio and the wireless mic from your subject. When you begin editing the project, you'll be able to mix these two channels to give your video a richer sound.

Lighting

When you purchased your camera, you should have purchased your camera light. Depending on the type of light you have, you should be able to attach the light on top of the camera where it can slide into what's called the shoe mount of the camera.

For most church weddings, you're not usually allowed to use any camera lights. Most modern cameras can handle relatively low-light situations without a light so this should not pose too much of a problem. When you get to the reception, that's when you're going to need the light. For most of your reception shooting, you should be fine having the light mounted on top of the camera. Be aware that when you conduct interviews with the guests, they may react to the light by commenting how bright it is. Unfortunately, unless you have plenty of light in the area that you conduct your interviews, you'll have to use it. You may decide to forewarn them though. Many videographers use only their one camera light for the entire reception.

Now you're ready to go.

Chapter 4
How to Use the Equipment

N ow it's time to learn how to use your equipment. I'll begin with the camera.

Using the Camera

Most of the professional and prosumer camcorders come with the ability to adjust different elements that affect the image quality you record. Learning and mastering these controls will become extremely beneficial to your productions.

Iris Control

The iris (see Figure 4-1) inside a camera's lens controls the amount of light (see Figure 4-2) that will be allowed to reach the camera's CCD (see Figure 4-3). The iris control of a camera works similar to the iris in your eyes. In bright conditions, the iris of your eye expands, making your pupil smaller in order to decrease the amount of light coming into your eye and onto your retina. When a camera is set to automatic iris control, the iris in the lens of the camera makes the opening smaller (see Figure 4-4), just like your eyes, to decrease the amount of light that will reach the camera's CCD chip or chips. Under bright light, a wide-open iris would overexpose the scene and create a very washed out look in your video, similar to watching an atomic bomb explode (see Figure 4-5). Under low light, the iris in your eyes open the pupils wide (making them appear larger) to let more light in. The camera's iris would do the same. If it didn't, your video would be under-

Figure 4-1
Iris of a
camera lens.

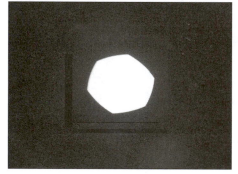

Figure 4-2
The iris controls how
much light is let into
the camera.

exposed and the video images would appear very dark and lose detail and color in the picture (see Figure 4-6).

In the automatic iris mode, video cameras evaluate every portion of the image coming through the lens in order to determine how much light to let in. If part of the image is really dark and another part is really bright, how does the camera determine which area to adjust for? The camera may react in different, unpredictable ways for each different lighting situation it is in. This is why we want to be able to override the automatic process and manually adjust the iris ourselves. If the subject we're trying to focus on is too dark, we can open the iris. If the subject is too bright, we can close the iris. **NOTE: Video cameras do not handle large differences between light and dark very well.**

Figure 4-3
The camera's CCD is located behind the lens inside the camera.

Handling Backlight Problems

When your subject is in a shaded or dimly lit area and the background is very bright or brightly lit, you have what is referred to as a backlight situation. In Figure 4- 7, the camera's iris was opened enough so that you could adequately see the subject. Unfortunately, the background is "blown out" or overexposed as I talked about earlier. In Figure 4-8, the background is appropriately exposed, but the subject is underexposed and hard to see.

There are three possible solutions for this problem. I'll use the image in Figure 4-8 as an example. First, I could move the subject to another location where the lighting is more balanced between the subject and the background, such as an area where both the subject and the background are shaded. (Refer to Figure 4-16 for an example of this method.)

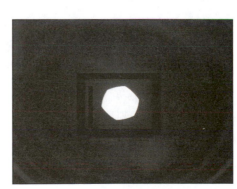

Figure 4-4
Smaller opening in the iris.

Figure 4-5
Overexposed image.

Figure 4-6
Underexposed image.

Figure 4-7
Subject is properly exposed; background is overexposed.

Figure 4-8
Background is properly exposed; subject is underexposed.

Second, I could use a light (or a reflector if I'm outdoors) in front of the subject, pointed right at them in an attempt to balance the lighting on the subject with the background lighting.

Third, I could move the camera to a different angle where the background is not quite as bright and bring the two lighting areas closer in brightness. Of course, if I do this, I will need to have the subject turn to face the camera or I may wind up shooting their backside.

Shutter Speed Control

When someone shoots a movie on film, their camera is taking a series of photographs in a short amount of time, usually around 24 pictures in one second for every second. When you show these photos in sequence at the same speed (24 frames per second), the subjects in the photos become animated. Just like movie cameras, video cameras also snap these series of photos. Behind the lens is a shutter that opens and closes very quickly, taking almost 30 photos per second. The shutter speed of the camera refers to the length of time the shutter stays open to capture each image (or photo). Most video cameras default to a shutter speed of 1/60th of a second.

For a beginner wedding videographer, I don't recommend adjusting the shutter speed. When you become more comfortable with the whole process, you may want to experiment later. I mention it here because you should be aware of it.

Focus Control

Many camcorders come with an auto focus feature. This is where the camera attempts to determine what to focus on and adjusts the focus accordingly. For example, let's say there are different subjects in your shot (or frame) and each is at a significantly different distance from your camera. Your camera will not be able to focus on all of them at the same time. So how does it know which subject you want to focus on? Most cameras will default to focusing on whatever's in the middle of the frame. If you did not want to focus on that particular subject, then you would have to move the camera so that the target subject is in the middle of the frame; this changes the composition of the shot. There is another way to accomplish your desired shot without changing the composition. You can override the automatic focus and manually adjust the camera to focus on the subject you originally wanted to highlight.

This really becomes important when you start setting up creative shots. You've probably seen a shot where the camera appears to be looking at something or someone through the bushes. You'll notice that even though it appears that we are looking through the bushes, the bushes are out of focus (blurry) and the subject is in focus (sharp).

You'll need to master this task quickly. A professional videographer always uses manual focus.

White Balance Control

If you're new to video, you're probably wondering, "What is white balance?" Most cameras will come with an automatic white balance setting where the camera tries to figure how the colors should be displayed. Unfortunately, video cameras are not as good as the human eye when it comes to detecting colors correctly. For a better understanding of what this is about, we need to talk about color temperatures.

Color Temperatures

When we say color temperature, we don't mean that colors have a fever. Color temperature refers to an assigned value (rated in degrees Kelvin) for each characteristic of color. For example, you're outdoors on a sunny day in the middle of the day. The color temperature is said to be a colder (more blue) temperature, say 5200K. When you're indoors under normal lamp lighting, the lights are more yellow and considered to be warmer (3400K). That's why your consumer camera's images tend to appear bluer when it films outside and more yellow inside.

Adjusting the Camera

We can adjust the camera's perception by putting a solid white subject in front of the camera and manually white balancing on it. This tells the camera, "Hey, this is true white; adjust your colors accordingly." When you take the camera outside during the day to do this, you'll notice the white object may look a little blue in color (see Figure 4-9). After you perform the adjustment, all of the

Figure 4-9
Outdoors, before white balancing the camera.

Figure 4-10
Outdoors, after white balancing the camera.

Figure 4-11
Indoors, before white
balancing the camera.

Figure 4-12
Indoors, after white
balancing the camera.

colors should look normal, without the bluish tint (see Figure 4-10). When you take the camera inside, under indoor lighting, your white object may appear yellow and everything in the room will have a yellowish tint (see Figure 4-11). Perform the white balance again and you'll see the camera adjust to make the white object appear white again and all other colors will look normal (see Figure 4-12).

Different lighting situations will produce different results with the camera. That's why we need to have the ability to adjust the white balance whenever it's necessary.

Gain Control

Most of the professional and prosumer cameras have the ability to manually adjust the gain. The only times you'll need to be concerned about adjusting the gain is when you're shooting in a low-light setting where there's not enough light, even with your camera light, to get a decent picture. Let's say you've opened your iris all the way and your camera light is on. You can see something in the picture, but it still looks very dark. At this point, you could turn the gain up, and that might give you an acceptable picture. The downside to using the gain control is that it adds noise or particles to the picture, degrading your picture quality the more you add gain. If you want to see how this works, practice in low light. Turn it up, turn it down, and record everything you do, then go look at what you've recorded on your video monitor.

Zoom Control

Every video camera has a zoom control. Some would argue whether that's a good idea or not, since it has become the most overused feature on the entire camera. The zoom control allows you to appear to move closer to or farther from your subject without you having to move at all. Amateur videographers tend to like to zoom in and out almost constantly. A true professional uses the zoom control sparingly and creatively.

The most common use of the zoom control is for what is called a pull or a reveal shot. This is where you zoom all the way in on your subject, focus the camera, start recording, then slowly and smoothly zoom out with the camera revealing the surroundings around your subject. It can be a very nice shot if performed correctly. Zooming in (also called a push) is not used nearly as often, since it does not offer much interest to the viewer in terms of creativity or telling the story.

For more information on these various camera controls, how they work, and how to use them, you may enjoy watching a video called *Camera Command*. This video is very well done and explains all of the intricacies of how a camera works in a very simple and easy-to-understand way. It includes several wonderful examples to show you the results of each adjustment. To order a copy, go to www.provideotraining.com.

Setting Audio Levels

Most of the professional and prosumer cameras have the ability to manually adjust the volume or audio levels. This will become important to know how to use in the future, so you may want to take out the instruction manual for the camera and learn how to set these. I will offer this tip: digital camcorders have zero as the highest setting on the meters for the sound. When you manually adjust audio, never let the loudest parts of the sound go past the –6 level on the meters. If it does, you'll need to turn the volume down. This can cause distortion in the sound later, and there's no way to fix distorted sound.

Composing Your Shots

This subject alone could fill a book or two. Mastering the art of composing shots can put thousands of dollars in your bank account. This is the one aspect of video production that truly separates the professionals from the amateurs. Here are a few tips to get you started.

There will be shots that need to be composed using symmetry. For example, look at Figure 4-13. The subject is off to one side, making the shot appear unbalanced. Now look at Figure 4-14. With the subject in the center of the frame, the shot looks symmetrical and balanced. The result is more pleasing to the eye. This type of composition works best when the subject is directly facing the camera.

When you are shooting someone who is not looking at the camera but off to the side of the camera instead, you should position the subject off to the side of the frame. In Figure 4-15 the subject is positioned in this way however,

Figure 4-13
Unbalanced frame.

Figure 4-14
Balanced frame.

it looks a little strange. You should always position the subject on the side of the frame opposite of the direction they are facing, as in Figure 4-16. Keep this in mind whenever you have a subject walking across your frame. You should always leave space in front of the person walking, so they can never walk out of your shot unless you want them to. If your subject is walking from one side of your frame towards the other, keep your camera moving in the same direction as they are and don't let them reach the other side of your frame. This is referred to as "leading them". And, of course, make sure your camera moves smoothly while you are doing this.

In order to be a true professional, you'll need to be familiar with the "rule of thirds." A simple explanation of the rule of thirds is to fill up two-thirds of your frame with your subject. To help you visualize this, I'll use the last two figures I just talked about. I'll draw two vertical and two horizontal lines across the image that will divide the picture into nine equal parts. Refer to Figures 4-17 and 4-18. Notice that the subject in Figure 4-17 fulfills the requirement of using two-thirds of the frame, but it still looks strange. In Figure 4-18, the subject fills two-thirds of the frame, but this time the picture looks better. For more information about the rule of thirds, check your local library for books on photography or search the Internet.

Here are a few more suggestions on how to improve your camera technique:

- Watch television and movies with the sound turned down and pay attention to how the cameras follow the action.
- When you are shooting a bride and groom close-up, make sure they're both in the shot and try not to cut off the tops of their heads. They won't like this.
- Pick up a copy of the *Advanced Broadcast Camera Techniques* video. There are a lot of great camera techniques in this video.

When to Use a Tripod

For a wedding, I recommend using a tripod for the entire ceremony. Any time you will be videotaping continuously for a long period of time, it's a good idea to use a tripod; your arms will get tired if you don't. A good time to use a tripod is when you need a nice steady shot, particularly when you have to zoom in a lot. The pre-ceremony events, post-ceremony events, and reception will

Figure 4-15
Incorrect framing
of shot.

Figure 4-16
Correct framing
of shot.

require you to be a lot more mobile, so a tripod may not be practical for these parts of the wedding day.

Chapters 9–11 will cover the specifics about what to videotape during the wedding day.

Using the Editing System

When it comes time to begin editing the video you've finished shooting, you'll need to understand the basics of how your editing system works. Since there are many editing systems out there, it will be too difficult to be very specific, but I'll attempt to address the basics. Chapter 12 will cover the specifics of how to edit the actual wedding video.

Capturing Video

The first step in the editing process is to capture the video into your computer. As mentioned previously, you should consult your editing software manual or consult with the dealer that you purchased your system from on how to accomplish this.

Opening Your Editing Software

The next step is to open the editing program and import the video clips you've captured.

Most editing programs will have a few different windows within them. Each window will contain one of the following: the video clips (after you've imported them), the available transitions, and the timeline. Each program may have a different name for these windows, but they should serve the same function. Some programs may have more windows than I've mentioned here, but these will be the most important.

Video Clip Window

One window should be dedicated for containing the videos clips you will be using for editing your project. Using your mouse, drag the video clips down to your timeline, placing them in the order you want them to appear, from left to right.

Figure 4-17
Rule of thirds,
incorrect framing.

Figure 4-18
Rule of thirds,
correct framing.

The Timeline Window

Most every editing program being used today utilizes what's called a timeline for editing. It looks like a set of rows, and it is usually located at the bottom of the screen. Once you have dragged your video clips onto the timeline, you'll be able to trim any extra video that you don't want, from the beginning and the end of each of the video clips. Some programs may allow you to trim the clips before you place them on the timeline. After you've put the clips on the timeline, you'll drag transitions down from the transition window. I always put some black at the beginning and the end of the video project on the timeline.

Transitions Window

Editing programs have a window that contains all of the transitions available to that program. A transition is a type of effect that takes the viewer from one video clip to another. For example, the most common transition used today is the dissolve. This is where one clip fades into the other. The transition window will contain many different kinds of transitions. I recommend that you try all of them to get familiar with how they look in your project. I suggest that you never use all of them on any one project that you edit for a client.

Finishing Touches

Once all of your clips have been trimmed and transitions have been placed, you're ready to add titles and music. I recommend having the person who sold you the system show you how to perform these operations. There are also many books and training videos available to help you use these various editing systems.

IMPORTANT TIP: More DVD players will be able to play DVD-R (referred to as DVD minus R) discs than any other recordable DVD format. Therefore, it is the most recommended disc type for recording DVDs.

After you've finished editing the video, it will be time to transfer it to your videotape or DVD. Most of your customers will be asking for DVD copies of their video. As mentioned in Chapter 2, there are two types of DVDs, authored and unauthored. Let's review them again. The unauthored DVD will play like a VHS videotape; you start at the beginning and play through the video. The standalone DVD recorders may automatically put chapter or index points on the disc about every 10 minutes or so. When playing the DVD, the only way to skip through the video is to either use the fast forward button or the chapter skip button that will skip through the video in the preset increments. The DVD will have a basic-looking menu.

The authored DVD has to be created on the computer. The disc will have chapter points wherever you put them. The menu will allow the viewer to skip to specific chapters of the video. You have the ability to customize the menu and make it look professional. In my opinion, the authored DVD is the preferred choice as it makes you look more professional, but it does take more time to create and therefore you should charge more for this type of DVD. I'll discuss more about this topic later.

Creating an Unauthored DVD

This process requires a stand-alone DVD recorder.

To create an unauthored DVD, I recommend transferring your edited video to a digital videotape first in case there's a problem during the transfer. If you attempt to transfer directly to DVD and there's a problem during the transfer, you'll have to throw the disc away and start over. If you transfer the video to digital tape first and there's a problem during transfer then, you'll be able to back the tape up and record over the previous recording, and nothing will be wasted.

The simplest way to transfer (or dump) the video to tape is to press Record on your VCR and start playing the timeline (consult your software manual on how to do this). After the video has been put on tape, you're ready to copy it to DVD.

Your DVD recorder should be able to connect to your digital VCR using either FireWire or RCA and S-Video cables. Make sure to set your DVD recorder to the appropriate input. You should cue the videotape up to the black at the beginning of the video and put the VCR into pause mode. Place a blank DVD-R in the DVD recorder and push Record. Once the recorder has started recording, push the Pause button on the VCR to release it from pause mode. You may want to write down how long the video is so that you will be ready to stop the DVD recorder at the end of the video.

After the video has finished recording and you've stopped the DVD recorder, you'll need to put a track title on the disc for the track you just finished recording. You may also want to put a disc title on the disc as well. Both of these procedures have to be done before finalizing the disc. The DVD has to be finalized before it will be able to play on any other DVD player. Refer to your DVD recorder's instruction manual on how to do this. Once the DVD has been finalized, it's ready to be labeled. Labeling the discs will be covered in Chapter 14. An unauthored DVD takes a few minutes longer to create than the actual length of the video. For example, a 90-minute video will take 90 minutes to record, a few minutes to title, and another few minutes to finalize. Total time is about 10 minutes longer than the actual length of the video.

There are a few disadvantages of making DVDs this way. First, the DVD recorders offer only a simple menu design that usually cannot be changed or customized. Secondly, the viewer is not able to go directly to any particular part of the disc. The disc is essentially played in order starting at the beginning and continuing to the end, similar to a VHS tape. Most DVD recorders will automatically place an index point about every 10 minutes or so that you can advance using the DVD player's Next button. And, finally, if you want separate chapters, then you'd have to stop recording at the end of one chapter and start recording again at the beginning of the next, continuing this process for every chapter that you want to appear on the menu.

Creating an Authored DVD

This process requires a DVD burner in the computer.

The first step in creating an authored DVD is converting (encoding) your video into MPEG-2. Many of the editing programs have an option for exporting the timeline into an MPEG-2 file. After you have created MPEG-2 files, you will need to open up your DVD authoring program. In this program, you will import the MPEG-2 files and create the menu or menus for the DVD. Refer to the product's instruction manual on how to do this. Once you've created all of the menus and laid everything out, put a blank DVD-R disc into your computer's DVD burner. You may then begin burning the disc. This process will automatically include the finalization process, so you don't have to worry about that. When the disc has finished burning, it's ready for labeling. Again, refer to Chapter 14 regarding this process. For authored DVDs, it takes about as long as the video length to encode the video into MPEG-2. It can take several hours to create the menu and another hour to burn the disc.

After you've tried to author a disc, you'll see why it takes longer to create than an unauthored DVD.

One of the biggest advantages of an authored DVD is you have the ability to create chapter points that the viewer may go directly to by selecting them on the menu so the viewer can jump to any part of the video that the menu allows. For example, they could go right to the vows portion of the ceremony, and then jump to the first dance portion of the reception without having to skip through all of the parts in between.

Practice, practice, practice. Get to know how to use your equipment well. Learn as much as you can about the software you have. The more you know the more creative your videos will be.

Chapter 5
Getting Experience

When it comes to learning how to videotape weddings, there's no substitute for hands-on experience. The question is, how do I get this experience?

Videographer Associations

Many of the cities across the country have a local videographer association. Most videographer associations meet once a month, and they exchange ideas and techniques on video production. It's a great place to network with other videographers, and you may even learn more about video production. Get to know the other videographers in your area. Ask them if they need any help. If you're serious about getting some experience, offer to help them for free. You can learn a lot this way. There are at least three ways to find an association near you.

ProVideo Training Web Site

One resource you may want to become familiar with is the ProVideo Training website which lists local associations across the country.

Internet Search

Another method for finding a local association is to just do a search on the internet.

Call Other Videographers

You could call other videographers in your area and ask them if they know of any local videographer associations in your area. While you're on the phone with them, ask them if they need any help.

Working for Free

I know this sounds counterproductive to shoot video for free when you're trying to start your new career, but it's the best way to get some experience under your belt. The more weddings you shoot, the better prepared you'll be for shooting the next one, and you'll have more demo material to show to prospective clients. Couples are more likely to hire you if they feel you have enough experience to do the job right. How do you find these events to tape for free?

Call Wedding Locations

When I was trying to get some practice, I went through the Yellow Pages and called various churches and wedding locations. I told them I was with a local video production company and that we were looking for a wedding to videotape free of charge to the wedding couple because we needed to check out some new equipment. Then I asked them if they had any weddings coming up soon where the bride and groom were not planning on hiring a professional videographer. (This is the most important question to ask because you don't want to intrude on another professional videographer's event. That may come back to haunt you later in your video career.) The person you're talking to may ask if it's okay if they can call you back. Say yes and thank them for their time. If they confirm that they do have a couple that fits your description, ask for the couple's phone number and call them.

When you call the couple, ask them the same way you did when you spoke with the other person. Tell them you're with a local video production company and ask them if it would be okay with them for you to videotape their wedding free of charge so you can check out your equipment. Tell them you'll even edit the video for free as well. If they say no, continue on to the next call. If they say yes, find out when their rehearsal is and tell them you will be attending so that you can check the layout, camera positions, and other factors.

After you've found out when and where the actual wedding is, make sure you have their names, thank them, and tell them you'll see them at the rehearsal.

Bridal Shows

I'll talk more about bridal shows in Chapter 6, but I want to mention that you can purchase a booth at a bridal show and have a drawing for a free wedding videotaping. Brides and grooms can stop by your booth and fill out a form to enter for a chance to win an entire wedding video. Make sure your form includes the wedding date, their names, addresses, phone numbers, and email addresses. Have a designated entry box on your table for them to drop the forms into. After the show is over, you can draw the winning entry and call them to tell them they've won. If, by chance, the entry you drew out is for a wedding that's a whole year away, you may consider offering a second free wedding video. This time, give it to someone who is getting married very soon. Call them up and tell them they've won. Get all of their wedding information and go shoot it.

Wedding Vendors

Contact other wedding vendors such as dress stores, florists, caterers, DJs, or bakeries, to see if they'd be interested in having a drawing offered to their customers for a free wedding video. Then you would proceed using the same methods described in the previous paragraph.

What To Do After You've Taped the Wedding

After you've videotaped the free wedding, do the best editing you can. When the video is ready, call the couple and schedule a time for them to see the video. You can do this at their place or yours, whichever you feel more comfortable. Insist on being present when they watch it. The reason I recommend this is that you need every opportunity you can get for receiving instantaneous feedback on how you did. While the couple is watching the video, watch them for reactions at various points during the video. This instant feedback will help you get better at determining what parts of your work need to improve and which parts are fine the way they are. Make sure the couple gets their copy of the video. You may even want to give them a few extra copies for their parents. You will increase your chance of referrals when more people see your work.

Other Events

You could apply some of these tactics to find some other types of events to videotape for free to get experience. Other events could include parties, reunions, or anniversaries.

After you've gained enough experience to be considered competent, you can start charging a small fee and gradually increase your fee as you improve your skills.

Learning Materials

I feel that books, videos, and seminars are priceless when it comes to learning a new trade. The first couple of years I was in the business, I went to every seminar I could find about the video business, everything from marketing to editing. There's so much to learn. I can tell you from experience that it took me over five years to learn the majority of what I needed to know to become successful, and that involved taking advantage of all of the training resources I could find. Without these resources, I can't image how long it would have taken to learn that much knowledge. Here are some helpful resources, including a few that have really helped me.

Books

Besides the one you're reading, there are other books out there on the various software programs available as well as production techniques. There are lots of books on the subjects of sales and marketing.

Videos

I personally recommend "Camera Command," "Advanced Broadcast Camera Techniques," and both of Randy Stubbs' videos—"Sounds Like Creative Video" and "From Ordinary to Extraordinary." The "Camera Command" video does a wonderful job explaining iris settings, shutter speeds, focal lengths, and other camera-related features. "Advanced Broadcast Techniques" demonstrates the various different types of shots and how to get more creative shots. Everything I learned from this video helped me book more jobs. For a complete list of recommended training materials refer to the appendix in the back of this book.

Seminars

In my city, the Chamber of Commerce has a Small Business Development Center that gives various seminars on everything from sales to getting free publicity for your business. Check your local business journal or newspaper for advertisements for upcoming seminars. Check with your local videographer association to see if anyone offers seminars on video production. Check your local community colleges to see if they offer any video-related classes. They offer seminars all year-round. You'll never learn everything there is to know.

Chapter 6
Marketing and Getting the Clients

In my opinion, this is the most important chapter of this entire book. If you can't get any clients, you'll be out of business. When you make this the number-one priority in your business, you'll be way ahead of your competition. Back when I started my business, I knew the importance of marketing. I learned as much as I could on the subject and allotted a substantial portion of my budget for advertising. I needed to get up and running quickly. By prioritizing the marketing, I surpassed many of my competitors within a few years. Many of them have since gone out of business. Before you can market successfully, you need to know what's going on in your market.

Market Research

Don't let the term market research intimidate you. The process isn't really that complicated. One of the easiest ways to find out what your competition is doing is by looking them up on the Internet. Some video companies will list their packages and prices on their web site. Another method involves going to a bridal show and picking up flyers from videographers' booths. Either method will help you get some idea of what you competition is selling and what they're charging for it.

When I started, I discovered that many of my competitors filled their brochures with video industry lingo that most brides wouldn't understand unless they were actually *in* the business. This is a very bad idea. Why would a bride shop at a business if she doesn't understand what the product is?

As you look over the various brochures, imagine that *you* are the customer. Pretend that you don't know any of the industry terminology. How would you interpret the material? Is it saturated with technological verbiage, or is it easy for anyone to understand? Do you understand every item listed? Did they create packages, or is everything being sold a la carte? Note the price ranges and what they include. What types of options or services do they offer?

Determining Packages and Options to Offer

As you may have noticed during your market research, there are many variations of packages being offered and several different options available.

Possible Options to Offer

Some of the most popular options you can offer to prospective clients are photo montages, love story videos, bride-getting-ready montages, and a highlights version of the wedding day. Let's go over what each of these consists of. I've included a more comprehensive list of options in Chapter 14.

Childhood Photo Montages

Childhood photo montages as in Figure 6-1 are where you have the bride and groom go through their family photos and select pictures of themselves from different times of their lives as they were growing up. It's okay if they want to include pictures of their family as well. Then they will need to pick out photos of the two of them together during the time they've been dating. This is where you'll need a scanner for scanning the photos. Next they will need to choose some music to go with these photos. You'll use your editing system to put the photos together with transitions and music. Don't forget to add an opening title.

The average photo montage contains around 50 to 60 pictures and lasts from three to six minutes. The final product would be added to the beginning

Figure 6-1
Childhood Pictures for
Montage

of their wedding video and can also be shown at their reception if they like. You should be aware that some people may refer to photo montages as "slide shows." I tend to stay away from using that term since I feel my montages are much more interesting than slide shows.

Love Story Videos

Love story videos are when you take the couple out to a scenic location and film them interacting with each other. Examples of possible locations include a beach, a park, or by a lake as in Figure 6-2. Be aware that most couples have never been involved in shooting a love story before so, you will need to direct them as to what to do. For example, you could have them stare into each other's eyes while you shoot close-ups of each of their faces individually. If you're at the beach, you could have them walk along the water's edge holding hands while shooting this from different angles. The key is to be creative. You should have at least 45 minutes to an hour's worth of interaction shots. Again, ask them for music to put with these clips.

You may also want to interview each of them separately and ask them questions like, "How did you meet? How did he propose? What did you first think of her?." After you've completed the videotaping, you'll return to your editing system to capture and edit this footage into a short five- to seven-minute video montage. It may resemble a music video. This video will also be added to the final wedding video and can be shown at the reception as well.

Figure 6-2
Love story
interaction shot.

Bride-Getting-Ready Montage

For this montage, you'll need to go where the bride will be getting ready. This could be at home, in her hotel room, or at a salon. You'll be videotaping clips of her getting her hair and makeup done, shots of her bridesmaids and family, and so on, for example in Figure 6-3. The idea is to capture the essence of what it was like for her to get ready for this big day. Have the bride provide music for you to use in putting together this montage. This montage would also be added to the final wedding video, but you will *not* be showing it at the reception.

Wedding Day Highlights

As you may have guessed, this is a fully edited, condensed version of the wedding day. You take the highlights of the day and edit them down to a 40- to 50-minute short-form version. I have always included the full-length edited version in their package as well. I feel there is some footage that won't make it into the short version, but the bride and groom will want to see it at some point in time, so I include it.

Figure 6-3
Dressing the bride.

Option Pricing

You may want to determine how much you would charge for each of these options in case someone wants to add one of these to a package. You should charge between $150 and $500 for each. All of them require editing time that you should be paid for. As you get better at doing them, you can raise the price.

Packages to Offer

Most wedding vendors offer a choice of packages for their services, and couples are used to this. I recommend having at least three packages but no more than four if possible. The main reason is that too many choices may confuse potential clients. As the saying goes, "A confused mind always says no." This means that if it's too difficult for them to make up their mind, they'll probably go somewhere else. Here are the factors to consider when creating your packages.

Length of Wedding Day Coverage

One of the strategies I use for determining my packages is how many hours of coverage they will receive. When I first started, I offered three to four packages. At least two of them included unlimited time on the wedding day. Unlimited time packages draw interest from brides, but be careful that you don't undercharge for them. It can be a grueling job, as you may end up shooting for over 10 hours, and there will be a lot of editing to go with that. My entry-level package offered six hours of coverage, and my other package included eight hours.

Here is a breakdown of the minimum number of hours necessary for the following wedding situations:

- Three hours—for ceremonies only plus some pre-ceremony preparations and post-ceremony photos
- Five hours—ideal for weddings where the ceremony is 30 minutes or less in length or the ceremony and reception are at the same location or very close to each other
- Seven hours—ideal for ceremonies that are longer than 45 minutes or the ceremony and reception are in different locations that are not close together
- Nine hours—ideal for ceremonies that are 60 minutes or longer and where there may be a two- to three-hour gap between the end of the ceremony

and the start of the reception; also ideal if you want to include more bride preparation coverage with the package

· Over nine hours—allowing for more in-depth coverage before the ceremony and all the way to the end of the reception

Quantity of Cameras to Be Used

For most weddings, especially church weddings, I recommend using a minimum of two cameras to videotape the ceremony and one camera for the reception. The main reason for using two cameras for the ceremony is the ability to capture as much of the event as possible. Weddings don't allow for a second chance if you missed something the first time. Most churches won't allow you to move around once the ceremony has begun. One camera is usually sufficient for capturing the reception. I'll talk more about this in Chapter 7. I'll cover the specifics on what to shoot in Chapters 9 through 11.

Opening Titles and Closing Credits

I typically include opening titles at the beginning of my wedding videos and wedding party credits at the end. I used to superimpose the wedding invitation scrolling over a scenic background. Now I use a title-generating program to recreate the text from the invitation and scroll that over a video background instead.

Quantity of Copies of Video

All of your packages have to come with at least one copy of the video. Most of your customers will want it on DVD. I used to include more copies of the video with the higher-priced packages. I recommend including at least three copies with your packages. You may want to use an unauthored DVD in your lowest package and authored DVDs in your higher packages. This gives your customer a reason to upgrade to a more expensive package.

Options to Include with Your Packages

Any of the four options mentioned earlier could be included with any of your packages. You could start with one of them in your second-from-the-lowest-priced package and add another one with each package upgrade.

Package Pricing

In the beginning, you'll be charging prices closer to the bottom range of your market. As you gain more experience and produce better-looking videos, you'll want to increase your rates.

Sample pricing for your packages could be as follows:

Package A—five hours of coverage for $500

Package B—seven hours of coverage plus one option for $700

Package C—nine hours of coverage plus two options for $1,000

Package D—unlimited time plus three options for $1,400

Remember, these are just sample prices and you should base yours on your current market. For whatever reason, customers tend to choose the middle packages the most, so try to make these your most profitable packages.

IMPORTANT TIP: In the eyes of the consumer, when all things appear to be equal among competitors, the customer will always choose the least expensive.

Levels of Clientele

There are different levels of clients you will attract based on your price, quality of videos and service. In the beginning, you'll be targeting the lower-end clients that are looking for very inexpensive video services. As you gain more experience and become better at your craft, you should start raising your prices. As you do, your target market will change from low-end to medium-level. When the quality of your work reaches award-winning caliber, you'll be ready to seek out the premium clientele. You may consider purchasing a better camera for taping these events, as I alluded to in Chapter 2.

Creating Your Brochure

After you have developed your packages and determined how much you want to charge, you'll need to create a brochure. The brochure should look nice and professional. It should contain a description of your packages along with any options you plan to offer and the price for each. Make sure your brochure is appropriately designed to address the market you wish to target. For example, upscale clients will expect a higher quality of brochure than the low-end clients.

Benefits vs. Features

Try to avoid using videographer terms as much as possible. You may be excited that you've learned what "three-chip" means, but your prospective client won't care. They want to know, "What can you do for us?" The bride is not interested in how many lines of resolution your camera has; she wants to know that you know how to capture Dad walking her down the aisle. Brides buy benefits, not features. You have to engage their emotions.

Creating Your Demo

Another important reason for shooting some practice weddings is to obtain footage that you can use for creating your demo video. Prospective clients will want to see samples of your work before hiring you. The quality of the sample you show them will have a strong impact on their decision of whether to hire you or not.

Checking Out Your Competition

As mentioned previously, there are a few methods for finding out what your competitors are doing on their demos. Many of them will hand out samples at bridal shows or have a sample on their web site. Often, videos are shown at local video association meetings. *Under no circumstances* should you call them or email them pretending to be a client and asking to have them send you a demo! Most videographers can tell when they're being shopped by competitors and are not likely to send out a demo. If they find out that it was you who was doing it, they're much less likely to offer to help you in the future. In other words, don't burn your bridges.

What to Put in Your Demo Video

Your demo video should contain footage from a wedding or weddings that you have videotaped. It could be a highlights version of a wedding that you've done or some clips from a few different weddings. Either way, I suggest making your demo no longer than 30 minutes if possible. You may wind up using it during your consultations with prospective clients for showing them samples of your work.

Make Your Demo Convey Your Style

The purpose of the demo video is to show potential customers what *your* style looks like, not your competitors'. For this reason, don't just copy what your competitors are doing. During my research, I discovered that almost every video I saw contained nothing but slow-motion footage of the same types of shots. After looking at several, I had a hard time separating one from the other. Guess what—if I had trouble, so will the brides. When brides can't tell the difference in videos, they'll usually go with whoever charges the least.

Don't Overuse Special Effects

My number-one policy when it comes to producing videos is "never overdo anything." By this I mean that if you want to use an effect, that's fine, but don't keep using it over and over and over throughout the video. People get tired of that. The videos that I watched containing nothing but slow-motion shots made a three-minute video feel like a 20-minute video. Slow motion is a nice effect for creating drama, but if every shot uses it then the impact is lost.

My Secret to Making Your Demo Stand Out

Here was my most important discovery during my research. *Not one demo* told the prospective customer why they should choose their company. I've had more success with demo videos when I included information on how to choose a videographer and why they should choose me. When I handed out my video at bridal shows, I received a 30 percent response for bookings! Marketing experts will tell you that any marketing that generates more than a 10 percent response is very good. If you'd like to order a copy of this demo, go to www.provideotraining.com.

Finding Your Clients Through Advertising

Now that you have your brochure and demo ready, it's time to find the customers. Here's another little secret I'll share with you. The secret to success in your business is to find a niche with little to no competition. When I started my business, all of my competitors focused on the brides who *were* planning to hire a videographer. I chose to focus my marketing attention to the brides who were *not* planning on hiring a videographer. Not one of them tried to market to these brides, so I had an exclusive market. Here are some of the possible channels for advertising and marketing your business.

Bridal Shows

Bridal shows are one of the most preferred ways of getting your name out there. Depending on the show, they tend to attract from 200 to 2,000 brides looking for wedding vendors. That gives you a lot of opportunities to reach potential customers. Make sure you have plenty of brochures and copies of your demo to hand out at the show. It helps to have a monitor and video player on display in your booth showing samples of your work. Try to dress up your booth and make it look warm and inviting.

If you bought a booth at a smaller show, try to spend some time talking with any bride or groom who comes to your booth. Ask them some questions about the wedding such as, "When and where is your wedding going to be?" The smaller shows give you more opportunities to build rapport with them, and that may help you get more clients.

As mentioned earlier, you may want to have a prize giveaway to encourage brides to fill out an entry form in order to win. The entry forms will provide you with contact information so you can continue marketing to them. After you've been in business for a few years and you've establish yourself in your market, you may decide to discontinue the giveaways, as they will be attracting the wrong type of bride for your services.

The biggest drawbacks for bridal shows may be the cost of the booth and the competitive environment. Expect to pay anywhere from $250 to $900 for a booth space. There are usually several other videographers competing for the same brides, and some of them may be offering low prices. All in all, I think it's still worth the investment, especially when you're trying to get started.

Direct Mail

Most bridal shows will offer you a mailing (or email) list containing the names and contact information for all of the brides or grooms who came to the show. You can use this information to send your brochures via mail or email. There's always a chance that you may have missed some of them during the show for whatever reason. Even if you did give them a brochure at the show, you can send them another one. This keeps your name on their mind. In fact, you may consider sending them a postcard every month or so until their wedding date to help them remember you. They say a customer needs to see your name an average of seven times before they'll buy from you.

Telemarketing

After you've received your contact list from the bridal show, you may choose to call brides and grooms to see if they need video. This will involve some time and a lot of rejections. I'm not a big fan of telemarketing, since I know what it's like to be on the receiving end of those calls.

Wedding Vendors

Networking with other wedding vendors is a great way to generate possible leads. Make an effort to contact them by phone, especially wedding coordinators. At bridal shows, the slow periods are great times to talk with the other vendors, starting with the ones around you. When you're videotaping a wedding, try to find some time to talk with the other vendors, get to know them and exchange cards. This could lead to referrals. However, don't do this during the moments when you or they need to be working. For example, you could talk with the DJ or photographer during the time when the guests are eating. Visit some bridal shops and meet the owners, managers, and help. Ask them if they'll let you put some brochures on their counter. Some vendors may already have another videographer that they recommend, but it's worth a try.

Bridal Magazines

I'm including bridal magazines in this book, because I feel you should be aware of them. I don't usually recommend them as they have not proven to be a very effective method for advertising wedding video production, in my experience. If you should decide to advertise in one, make sure it's a local magazine. National bridal magazines are very expensive and don't yield good results for attracting local brides. You'll need to develop an ad that generates interest and makes them want to contact you. Otherwise, it's just money down the drain.

Some bridal magazines may include a mailing list of brides with their advertising package. You can use this list similar to the way you'd use the bridal show list.

Newspaper Ads

I don't recommend newspaper ads either. For newspaper advertising to be effective usually requires repetition, and that can get real expensive in a hurry. Plus, most brides don't shop for wedding vendors in the paper. Similar to the magazine ad, if you want to try the newspaper, you'll need an ad that gets their attention and makes them want to contact you.

TV and Radio

TV and radio can offer some great exposure, but they're usually expensive. I don't recommend them while you are getting started.

Yellow Pages

Placing an ad in the Yellow Pages might get you a few calls for wedding videos. Usually you'll receive calls from brides who are looking for a videographer at the last minute and for a low price. You are required to pay for the ad every month, and you're obligated for an entire year until the new book comes out. And the cost of the ad seems to go up every year.

Internet

I can't leave this section without mentioning the Internet. It seems in today's business world you have to have a web site. It can be a great resource for attracting clients. You can put your brochures and sample videos on your site for brides to check out anytime they like, 24 hours a day, 7 days a week. It costs as little as $120 a year to have a company host your web site. If you want someone to design your site, that will cost more, usually about $45 to $65 an hour or more for their time. Your site should be rich with helpful information about wedding video *and* why they should hire you. It should be aesthetically pleasing to the eyes and easy to navigate around. You will need to obtain a domain name and then register it with all of the major search engines, such as Google and Yahoo.

Once you have your web site up and running, you may consider advertising with some of the wedding-related web sites such as weddingconnections.com, theknot.com, and weddingsolutions.com. You can do a search on the Internet for similar sites in your area. You'll find that your web site will give you the most bang for your buck in terms of advertising. It's the least expensive form of advertising with the largest outreach of any other method. The only drawback is that you need to promote it in order for it to be effective. Make sure you list your web address on *all* of your promotional materials, business cards, and brochures.

Which Advertising Methods Are the Best?

I high recommend bridal shows, direct mail, and a web site. Of course, I always encourage networking with other vendors whenever possible. In the course of running your business, you may come across some unique or different ways to advertise. I'm not going to say that you should avoid them, but carefully consider whether or not a bride might seek a vendor using this medium. I would suggest putting aside a little money every year to use for experimental marketing, and don't try to do a bunch of it at once. Maybe try one new method every year. Do *not* discontinue doing any of the other methods that *are* working for you!

Chapter 7

Phone Calls and Appointments

Now that you've done your marketing, it's time for the next phase, the phone calls and appointments (or consultations). If you've done a good job with your advertising and marketing, you should start to receive phone calls from prospective clients at some point. If you had a booth at a bridal show, the calls should start coming in within the next few weeks. If several months have gone by from the time your advertising reached the prospects and you're still not receiving any calls, then it's possible that your ad didn't work. If this happens, you may want to read the previous chapter again or pick up a book or attend a seminar on marketing. For the purpose of this chapter, we're going to assume your ad worked and your phone has started to ring.

Phone Calls

When a prospect calls they'll usually start out by saying, "I'm getting married and I want some information about your services," or "how much do you charge?" Before you continue, you should ask their permission to ask them some questions. For example, if they start with a question, you may want to say something like, "Before I can answer that, I need to ask you a few questions. Would that be okay?" They will usually say yes.

Questions to Ask

Here are some questions to start with:

- When are you getting married?
- Where is the ceremony?
- Where is the reception?
- How many guests are you expecting?
- What time does the ceremony begin?
- When does the reception end?

This information will be useful in determining if you're available to shoot their wedding, how far you'll need to travel, what type of package will fit their needs, and so on.

There are three possible scenarios that will determine how to continue:

1. They haven't seen any of your work yet.
2. They saw the demo you handed out.
3. They've seen enough of your work that they don't need to see anymore.

For scenarios 1 and 2, proceed to the Scheduling the Appointment section. For scenario 3, they may already be interested in hiring you but maybe they still have a few questions to ask. If they have some questions, go ahead and answer them. If you need to ask a few more questions, go ahead. When all of the questions have been answered, you may want to ask them if they are interested in hiring you. If they say yes, proceed to the section on **Writing Up the Contract**. If they say, "I'm still checking around," then you can try asking them, "Is there anything else you need from me?" Or "Do you have any other concerns that we need to discuss?" If not, then you'll just have to wait to see if they call you back.

Scheduling the Appointment

If you don't already have one, I strongly encourage you to get a day planner of some sort that will allow you to keep track of your appointments and weddings. I know I'm lost without mine. I have a motto, "If it's not written down in my book, it's not happening."

Now it's time to ask them, "Would you like to set up a time to meet so I can show you some sample videos and answer any questions you may have?" If they answer yes, then find out what day is convenient for them. Have your appointment book handy so you can make sure you're available. Once you've narrowed down the day, ask them, "Morning or afternoon?" Many professionals recommend that you give them two choices for time slots so, you might say, "Would 10 o'clock be okay, or would 11 be better for you?" Now that you've set the day and time, you'll need to decide whether to meet at their home or yours.

Your Place or Theirs?

Most wedding videographers work from their home. Some choose to go to the client's home; others have the client come to them. If there's some reason why you don't want them to come to your home, then you'll want to meet at their home. When you go to their place, dress professionally, have your materials organized, and *be on time*! These three items will help convince them that you are professional. You don't necessarily have to wear a suit or a dress. I suggest dressing business casual, consisting of a nice pair of pants and a polo-type shirt for men and a blouse with a skirt or slacks for women.

If you do meet them at your home or office, then make sure your place is neat, clean, and organized. You'll want to present a professional appearance whenever possible and have your materials organized. I always had extra copies of my brochure ready in case they needed a copy. I had a video sample in the player, cued up and ready to show. And I had a contract handy in case they decided to hire me. As they say, you have only one chance to make a first impression.

When I started my company, I worked from my home. I kept my living room very neat, clean, and presentable for clients coming in for consultations. I quickly discovered that editing videos and trying to run my business took a lot of my time. I found I could save a lot of time if I didn't have to run all over town for appointments. So by having them come to me, I could schedule one appointment right after the other.

This reminds me of when I started my business. My wife and I were renting a house in sort of a run-down neighborhood where the houses were old and the lawns were half dead. When a potential customer drives into this type of neighborhood, their expectations are immediately lowered. (Strike One.) Previous owners of my home had decided to convert the living room into a bedroom and build a new living room onto the back of the house. Why was this a problem? You had to enter the house from the back yard. So, when the prospect arrived in front of my house, they would immediately notice that we had no front door, and that's not very welcoming. (Strike Two.) Then, as soon as they entered the house, they might see a messy kitchen as soon as they came in. (Strike Three.) I could have three strikes against me before I was even able to show them any of my work.

Two years later, we bought a newer home in a nice neighborhood. So when they drove into our neighborhood they would think, "Nice neighborhood." When they pulled up in front of the house they would think, "Nice house, this videographer must be a good one if he can live here." After entering the front door they would see a nice and neat living room. By the time we sat down to watch a video, the prospect was two-thirds sold on me just because of the image they've built in their mind based on what they've seen so far. In the previous house, I had to overcome any uneasy feelings they may have had about me based on where I lived. The newer home made it much easier to close sales.

The Appointment

Now it's time for the appointment. You're dressed professionally, brochures in hand, and ready to go.

Breaking the Ice

This is a good time to remember that your prospect is probably as nervous about this appointment as you are. It will be your job to put them at ease. You may want to ask them easy questions like, "How is your wedding planning going?" or "How long have you and your fiancée known each other?" or "How did you two meet?" This will show them that you're interested in them and their situation. Watch for opportunities to empathize with them. Try to avoid any questions that may invoke fear, anxiety, or include the word "nervous," such as "Are you nervous about the wedding?" These types of questions evoke unhappy emotions. You want them to be experiencing happy emotions. People buy when they're happy. Make sure you ask your questions with a genuine interest. Don't try to fake it—they'll always know.

More Questions

Continue asking questions that will help you determine what they are looking for in a videographer. Make sure you listen to their answers. You may even want to ask them if it's okay if you take notes. They usually like this; it shows you're interested and professional. Here are a few more examples:

· Have you seen any other wedding videos?
· If yes, was there anything in those videos that caught your interest?
· Was there anything in those videos that you really didn't like?
· Do you like slow-motion, black and white, or any other effects in your video?
· Is there anything in particular that you have to have in your video?

When you've finished asking your questions, ask them if they have any questions for you. At some point in the conversation, you'll want to tell them the benefits of working with you or why they should hire you. Don't sound like you're begging for their business, just state these items as simple facts.

Showing Your Video

After all of the questions have been answered, ask them if they would like to see a sample. Most of them will say yes. You should already have prepared a sample video for them to watch. I have always used a 30-minute highlights version from one wedding. That way they'll have an idea of what to expect their video will look like. I'd stay away from showing a video that contains a bunch of random clips from different weddings. Now, start the video. Try not to talk at all while they are watching unless you absolutely have to. Let them absorb it all.

Explaining Your Packages

When the video is over, ask them if they have any more questions for you. If you haven't already done so, go over your packages with them and explain what they include and what the differences are between the various packages. Tell them about the options you offer and show them samples of these options if you have any. When it comes to video, brides won't buy options if they don't know what they look like. For example, if you plan to offer the "bride getting ready" option and you have not videotaped one yet, you may consider offering to do one for free so that you'll have a demo to show future prospects. Make sure they understand your packages and options and what is included.

Closing the Sale

Most videographers are not comfortable with closing the sale. They feel they are videographers, not salespeople. Here's a little secret—you don't have to be a salesperson to close a sale. All you have to do is ask. Here's what I mean. When you've finished showing the video and all questions have been answered, it's time to find out how you did. First, I'd start with, "What did you think of the video?" When they answer, watch their body language. Often, you can tell when someone is lying. If they imply that they liked it, then follow up with this easy question, "Would you like me to reserve your date?" There are four possible ways they may answer this question: yes, by asking another question, we're not sure yet, or no.

1. If they reply with a "yes," tell them, "Great. Let's fill out the agreement." Then proceed to the section on Writing Up the Contract.

2. If they answer your question with another question, like "What would we have to do to reserve the date?" then your reply would be, "I just need to collect a deposit of $200 (or whatever your deposit amount is) and have you sign an agreement." If they decide to go ahead and hire you, proceed to the section on Writing Up the Contract. If not, they may say something along the lines of, "We want to think about it" or "I need to talk it over with my fiancée." In this case, proceed to answer no. 3.

3. If they answered with something along the lines of "We're not sure yet," or "We still need to think about it," or "We still have to meet with another videographer or two," then your reply will be something like, "I understand. This is an important decision to make. Would you like me to check back with you in a week?" If they say yes, then call them in a week. If they say, "No, we'll get back with you," thank them for their time and wish them

luck with the rest of their planning. If you like, you may tell them you'll hold their date for one week without a deposit. If you haven't heard from them after a week, the date will no longer be reserved for them. I've had clients contact me months later to hire me. If I was still available then, they would book me. If not, then it's not my fault, but I gave them the opportunity.

> **IMPORTANT TIP:** If you've done a good job of asking the right questions and you've provided a good presentation, then you've earned the right to ask for the sale.

4. If they answered no, then ask them, "May I ask why not?" They may give you an answer similar to answer no. 3. If they do, follow the steps for answer no. 3.

If they don't, they may not have liked your style of video. That's okay. Don't expect to book every prospect you see. There are many reasons why someone may not hire you. Remember, they are evaluating your personality, professionalism, quality, and style. If any or all of these do not match what they are looking for, they'll keep looking.

After several appointments, you'll start to get the hang of how to handle this part of the appointment. There are no absolute right or wrong ways to do it. *Remember this:* If you've done a good job of asking the right questions and you've provided a good presentation, then you've earned the right to ask for the sale. Salespeople have lost thousands of dollars by *not* asking for the sale.

Negotiating

Many people are not comfortable with negotiating. Some even hate it. It is a skill worth mastering, as it can increase your income substantially and save you a lot of money over the course of your life. It probably won't be necessary with most of your clients, but you will have a few instances when it will become mandatory. Here are a few tips that may help you with this process.

When They Ask for a Discount or Want More for Nothing

When the prospect asks for a discount or wants you to throw something in without a reason, never give in to their request too quickly. That's a sign of weakness. Here's an example of a possible consequence of giving in too soon. A client wants the videographer to take $100 off the price of the package the client is interested in. The client says, "If you knock $100 off of package B, I'll sign the agreement today." The videographer is anxious to book the job, so he eagerly agrees. Six months later, the client realizes that the package they chose doesn't have enough hours of coverage so, the client asks, "I really want to get some footage of the bride before the ceremony. Do you think you could go ahead and shoot that as part of our package?" The videographer is happy to have the client, so he says yes without adding anymore to the bill. When the video is completed, the client says, "I can't remember how many copies of the video we were supposed to get but, can you give us five copies? My parents are divorced, and I want to give each one of them a copy and one for a grandparent, too." The videographer doesn't want to risk upsetting the client, so he agrees.

Let's take a look at what happened. The client received $100 off a package that originally cost $1,100. The original package included eight hours of coverage, but the videographer ended up shooting for 10. The extra two hours of shooting resulted in an additional six hours of editing. Then the client wanted five copies of the video instead of the three that were included as part of the original package. The net result? The client received about $300 worth of upgrades for $100 less than the package was supposed to sell for. Considering that the original package price was set with a narrow profit margin in order to be competitive, the videographer actually lost money on the job and had to put in more work on top of that.

Was it worth it? Many might argue that this client will end up referring many more prospects due to the "deal" this videographer gave the client. Here's the problem with that argument. Most clients who continue to ask for more and more almost never refer anyone. They think only of themselves. If they do actually refer someone, that person is very likely to want the same kind of deal their friend received. Would you really want this kind of business where you keep losing money?

In summary, when you give in too quickly, customers will continue to push to see how much more they can get from you. I had a client that tried to get me to reduce my price by as little as $50. I firmly said no, that's the price. The client hired me anyway. If the client ever tried to get anything else, I always said no. That ended the ongoing negotiations. By the way, I watched this client continue to push for, and sometimes get, more concessions from the other wedding vendors. Needless to say, they had a bad experience with this client. My experience was okay and I made a profit. That's what we're in business for. Most clients understand this, so don't be afraid to do what is necessary to make a profit.

When Should You Give In to the Client?

There are times when you can be flexible, such as in situations when the client is asking for a reasonable request and they've shown that they are a good client. For example, if they referred another client to you and that client booked you, then you may want to honor the client's special request or add something of value to their package. I always try to take care of my good clients.

Another instance might be if you really messed up something with their video. For example, if you promised the client you'd have their video finished in two months and it took four to five months for you to finish it, you might want to give them something extra like throwing in some extra copies of the video. You may want to give them what they ask for as long as they have a reasonable request that won't add a significant amount of work or additional cost to the project. I'll cover what to do in problem situations in Chapter 16 on handling problems.

Writing Up the Contract

Rule number one: Don't ever use the term "contract" with a client; always refer to it as an "agreement." It sounds much less threatening to the client. You want them to feel as comfortable as possible when you get to this stage. The word "contract" makes people think of lawyers, and when they think of lawyers, it takes them to a negative state of mind, and we don't want that. I've included a sample agreement on the DVD.

VALUABLE TIP: How do you know if you have a good client? Common indicators include they treat you nicely; they are genuine, down-to-earth, nice people; they are friendly and warm-hearted; they show gratitdude for what you've done for them; and they refer clients to you.

Customer and Wedding Information

Now it's time to fill out the agreement. First, get all of their contact information, including the bride and groom's names, a full address, phone number, cell phone numbers, and email addresses. Write down their wedding date, ceremony start time, ceremony location, and reception location. Be sure to write down the date you're writing this contract and how they heard about you. It's very important for you to track where all of your business comes from. This will help you determine the best use for your advertising dollars.

Package Description and Options

This section of the agreement is very important as it is designed to protect both you and your client by clarifying what is expected from you. Before you can continue, you'll need to determine the appropriate package and option configuration to fit your client's needs and preferences.

Let's start with how many cameras to use for taping the wedding. As I mentioned in Chapter 6, I usually recommend at least two cameras for the ceremony and one for the reception. Here's why: In a church environment, camera 1 (often referred to as the front camera) is usually positioned at the front of the church off to the right side of the altar area (see Figure 7-1). This camera angle will allow you to have the best view of the ceremony processional, the couple's faces for most of the ceremony, and the bride's face during the vows when she's facing the groom. You may also be able to obtain some good shots of the bride's family and some of the guests from this angle.

Camera 2 (referred to as the back camera) is usually positioned at the back of the church, either on the side of the aisle (sometimes behind the last row of pews) or in the balcony. From this angle, you'll have the best view of the minister, scripture readers, profiles of the bride and groom during the vows, the recessional, and, occasionally, the soloist or musicians.

I have offered my customers the option of adding a third camera for the ceremony. Camera 3 can be used in many ways. You could position it at the front of the church off to the left side of the altar area (see Figure 7-2). This position offers the best view of the groom's face during the vows. You may also be able to get some good shots of the groom's family and some of the guests that camera 1 is not able to get. This position offers a different perspective of the couple during the ceremony as well. A third camera could also be used for getting other creative shots by having that camera move around during the ceremony, if possible.

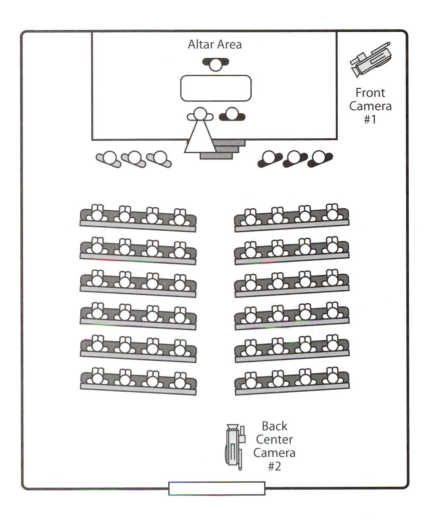

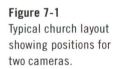

Figure 7-1
Typical church layout showing positions for two cameras.

Since most churches don't like the videographer to move around much, having at least two camera positions is vital for capturing all of the important parts of the ceremony. The same camera-angle benefits mentioned previously can also apply to outdoor weddings. Many outdoor weddings will have rows of chairs set up similar to church pews, with an aisle down the middle. It can pose a challenge trying to move around during the ceremony, trying to get all of the angles with just one camera.

Having a second camera to help cover the reception can be useful, too. It allows you to get crowd reaction shots for all of the action the first camera is capturing. You can use it to get different angles on the activities of the reception as well. Adding a third ceremony camera or a second reception camera allows for better and more complete coverage of the event, but you definitely need to charge more for them as you'll have to pay someone to operate the extra camera and more editing time will be required.

After you've discussed the various camera options with your client and they've made their decision on how many they want, you'll want to determine how many of hours of coverage they will need to ensure that you capture all of the activities of the wedding day that are important to them. The information you've gathered so far should help you determine the appropriate package for them.

If you haven't already done so, you should go over the various options you offer, show them samples, and find out which options the client is interested in. Once the package and option decisions have been made, you'll want to list everything that is to be included in the package on the agreement. In the actual agreement, you may refer to an attached brochure for the package description if you don't want to list everything out. Include any and all options they have chosen. On my agreements, I have boxes that they can check as to which package and options they want, and I will write in how much time is included in the package, how many copies of the video they are to receive and so on. These fields are very important to fill in as they'll keep the customer from trying to get more than they paid for.

Disclaimers

The "fine print" of the document, often referred to as the disclaimers, is very important for protecting you by reducing your risk of a lawsuit. Before I can continue, I must state my disclaimer.

Disclaimer: I am not an attorney, and therefore I cannot offer legal advice. I highly recommend that you consult your attorney regarding the legalities of any and all portions of any contract you enter into with your clients.

That being said, here are a few items I might suggest for you to put in your agreement. On the DVD, I have included a copy of a sample agreement that

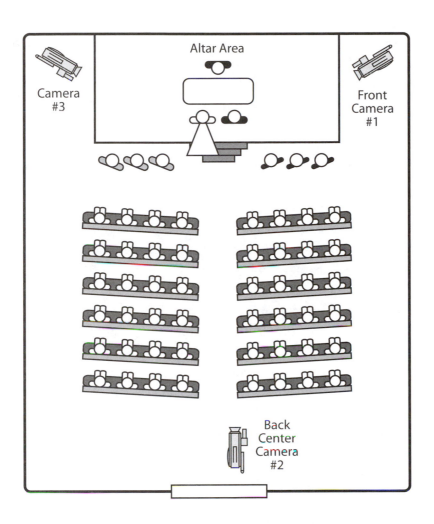

Figure 7-2
Typical church layout showing positions for three cameras.

I've used many times. My disclaimers are numbered from 1 to 7. Let's go over them.

1. Simply states the length of coverage my client will receive as part of the package they've chosen.

2. I'll request that I (and my crew, when applicable) am provided with a meal. I include this request for a few reasons:

   · As a videographer, I will be putting in a lot of hours on the wedding day and will need to eat at some point in time. Having them provide a meal will keep me from needing to leave the premises in search of food and therefore reduce the risk of my missing something important to videotape.

· When couples have reserved a caterer to provide food for their guests, they are required to provide the caterer with a final count of how many guests they will be expecting in order for the caterer to determine how much food will be necessary. Since the caterer has to order and prepare the food to accommodate the number of guests specified, the couple will be charged for all of those meals. In my experience, most weddings seem to have a few guests who say they are coming and then something comes up and they can't make it. This leaves a few meals that have been paid for but won't be consumed. Instead of letting it go to waste, why not feed the vendors, videographers, and photographers? I don't specify what the meal has to be, so if they want to provide a sandwich, that's fine with me.

My crew usually consists of me and either an assistant or a second cameraperson if the package calls for it. I also specify that we need to be allowed sufficient time to eat.

3. The next clause in my contract simply states that my company is the only official videographer of the event and that we have the right to let other people with video cameras know when they are in our way.

4. I want to let the client know that if they're not happy with my editing of their video and want to start requesting to have portions of the video re-edited, then they'll have to pay extra for it. This keeps the clients from being tempted to continuously make you re-edit the video over and over just because they're real picky. So far, in my career, this hasn't been an issue.

5. I need to let them know that the initial deposit I collect, in order to reserve the date, is not refundable. Once I have committed a date to a client, I will turn down any future prospects wanting my services for that date. If the client decides to cancel my services two weeks before their wedding, I will have lost all of those opportunities to book another event on that day, so I will lose money. That's why I'm entitled to keep the deposit. Most of the other wedding vendors also have this policy, so this should not be an issue.

6. I want to let them know that I will do my best to ensure that my equipment operates correctly, but I can't be responsible if it fails due to something beyond my control. Therefore, I am limiting my responsibility to the amount

that the client has paid me and no more. In other words, in the worst-case scenario I will give them all of their money back but no more than that.

7. Finally, I am letting the client know that (just like photographers) I own the copyrights to the final video. I will keep the edited master, and I have the right to show the video as a demo to future prospects or use it any way I choose. Even though I have the rights to use the video any way I want to, I probably would not send any of the footage into one of those TV shows like *Americas Funniest Videos* without the client's consent. It just makes good business sense.

The last line of the disclaimer section was designed as an attempt to discourage the client from making a bunch of copies of the video and not buy any additional copies from me. This point is not as important to me as it used to be. It seems that no matter what you do, you'll never be able to completely discourage your customers from making their own copies of the video. This is especially true with today's technology, making it even easier to make copies of DVDs. A fellow videographer and good friend of mine brought a very important point to my attention recently. He says instead of haggling over the few extra dollars you should have received from your client for extra copies of the video, you should give them the extra copies at no charge. He feels that giving out the extra copies increases the chances of more people seeing his work and it also makes for good P.R. as the clients will like you even more.

Balance Due and Deposits Paid Section

The next section of the agreement lists the amount the client is paying for the package they've chosen, the sales tax amount, total, the amount of the deposit they have paid, the balance that will be due (after the deposit has been subtracted), when the balance is due, and what form of payment they used for the deposit.

My policy for collecting payments is to collect a deposit when they sign the agreement to secure the date. The rest of the balance is due two weeks prior to the wedding. I have two reasons for this. One, the last week before the wedding is a very hectic week for the couple as relatives and friends start arriving in town, and they have a lot of last-minute details to take care of. With all of this going on, I want to make it easier on the couple and would rather not add my final payment to the list. Two, if they choose to pay by check, I'll have two weeks to make sure the check clears before I go out to shoot the wedding.

Some videographers choose to split up their payments into three payments. The first one is the deposit and the second (due prior to the wedding) will make up the difference between the deposit and 75 to 80 percent of the total. The final payment is due when the video is delivered to the client and represents about 20 to 25 percent of the total. Many videographers prefer this method since; it provides an incentive to finish editing the video. The only drawback I see is that if the couple should divorce before the video is completed, you would never see the final payment as they would no longer be interested in receiving the video. If you think this never happens, I know at least one videographer this has happened to.

The choice of how you collect is up to you, but I strongly recommend that you receive at least 75 percent of the total prior to the wedding so, in case your client decides to flake on you, you will have at least covered your costs.

Methods of Payment

No discussion on payments is complete without talking about what methods of payment to accept. The obvious methods you should be willing to take are cash and check. If you follow the guidelines mentioned in the previous section, you should be somewhat protected from suffering losses due to bounced checks, since you won't be shooting the wedding until you've received most of the payments.

I strongly encourage accepting credit cards. Customers who make larger purchases are more likely to use a credit card, and customers who use credit cards are more willing to spend larger amounts. This fact will come in handy as your prices rise. In order to accept credit cards, you will need to sign up for a merchant account through a credit card-processing company. Processing companies may charge an application fee, annual fee, or monthly fee. You may have a choice of either purchasing a credit card terminal or leasing one. And, all processing companies will charge a transaction fee for each purchase you process through them. These fees usually range as follows:

- For Visa, MasterCard, and Discover, between 1.5 and 3 percent of the transaction amount.

· For American Express, between 3 and 3.5 percent of the transaction amount.

The easier you make it for your client to do business with you, the more likely they will. I feel it's well worth paying these fees to get the business. Besides, all you need to do is just raise your prices enough to absorb the cost. That's what all other businesses do now. I currently accept all four of the major credit cards.

Client Signature

The final part of the agreement is where the clients sign, acknowledging that they have read and agreed to all of the terms of the agreement. They should also fill in the date next to their signature indicating the date it was signed. As long as your company's name and information appear somewhere on the agreement, you don't necessarily have to sign it. Some videographers do. It's up to you.

Unusual Situations

I've had clients who were ready to reserve my services for their wedding but were not ready to commit to a specific package. They wanted more time to think about what package they wanted. I told them that was fine and that I would just get their contact info and signature, write down their deposit on the agreement, and that we'd fill in the rest of the package information later when they decided.

Keep in mind that everyone has different situations and circumstances surrounding their event, so be as flexible as you can. Being flexible will help you book more weddings.

A Final Word on Contracts

The more information you have in your agreements the less confusion there will be on the services you're providing and there will be a lower probability that you'll end up in court. *Get it in writing!*

Chapter 8
Preproduction Planning

Now that you've booked the client, you'll have some planning to do over the next several months. One of your top priorities will be to find another camera operator or two, depending on the package you've sold.

Locating Additional Camera Operators

Unless you were able to afford two cameras, you'll need to find a camera operator who owns their own camera. If you don't already know a professional videographer who has a camera, you may consider joining your local videographer association and attending their meetings. Through this network, you should be able to find competent camera operators to help you document the event. I recommend seeing samples of their work before you hire them, if possible. Ask for references; maybe someone else in the association has used them before.

Getting a Commitment

Once you have found someone who is willing to help you, get a commitment from them if you can. You'll need to be aware that other videographers may book their own weddings and may not want to commit themselves to you at the expense of losing an entire wedding package of their own. If they don't want to commit to you right away, ask them how soon before the event would they be willing to commit. If the time frame they offer is acceptable for you, don't forget to contact them again when that time comes. Sometimes, it may be beneficial to check in with them every so often to remind them, but don't harass them. It's common for videographers to not want to commit their time to another videographer more than a month before the event.

Remember to ask them what type of tape their camera uses. You'll need to know this so you can have a blank tape available for them when they arrive at the ceremony. I never want to risk having a camera operator show up who forgot to bring a tape.

The Issue of Subcontractor vs. Employee

This topic alone could probably fill an entire book. When you hire someone to shoot a wedding with you, you'll need to be aware of the laws regarding their status in relationship to your company. Some videographers hire an employee that they use for their second cameraperson at weddings. As long as they're set up as an employee, then nothing further needs to be done. Most videographers hire subcontractors to be their second cameraperson. This means that this cameraperson has their own business which consists of shooting for their own customers or shooting for other videographers. As long as one or both of these are true, they will be considered a subcontractor. According to the law, if they work only for you they are not a subcontractor, even if they have their own business name.

Why is this important? If you hire a subcontractor and pay them like a subcontractor (meaning you don't withhold income tax or pay employer taxes) and they work only for you, the government may come in and say they need to be treated like an employee and that you must pay all employer taxes on this person plus interest and penalties.

One additional requirement for them to be considered a subcontractor is that you need to have a written agreement between the two of you for the job they are being hired for.

Using a Wedding Questionnaire

One of the most useful tools I've developed for my wedding business is a wedding day questionnaire. I typically send it out to my couples about a month before their wedding. If you send it sooner than that, they tend to lose it. A month before the wedding is the best time as the couple is just beginning to think about the details of the wedding and they will be meeting with their photographer and DJ soon to discuss the schedule for the day. My questionnaire is about four pages long and asks the important "need to know" questions about the wedding day and the type of coverage they're looking for. Here are some of the sample questions:

- When is the rehearsal?
- What is the address of the ceremony and reception?
- What is the name of the ceremony coordinator?
- How long is the ceremony?
- Will there be a full mass or any scripture readings?
- Are there any unique activities planned that I should know about?
- Do you want interviews?
- Will there be a toast? Father-bride dance? Bouquet and garter toss?

Once they have completed the questionnaire, have them send it back to you at least a week before the wedding. Review their answers, and if you have any questions, you can call them or you can schedule an appointment for them to come by and go over the details with you. The more you know about the wedding day plans, the better prepared you'll be for capturing the important moments. I will then take the questionnaire with me on the wedding day and keep it in my pocket throughout the event. It serves as a reminder so I don't forget any of the details we've discussed. On the last page or two, I will ask for the names of the wedding party and anyone else they wish to have listed in the closing credits of the video. There's a sample questionnaire on the DVD that you can use as a guideline for developing your own.

Trying Out New Equipment

If you need to purchase a new piece of equipment for use at your next wedding, limit your equipment purchase to one new item. Try to avoid experimenting with more than one new piece per event. Make sure you test out the new equipment and fully understand how it works before using it at an actual event. There's enough stress involved in taping a wedding without adding more unnecessarily.

Attending the Rehearsal

Attending the rehearsal is a very important part of the preproduction process. It provides a great opportunity to become familiar with the ceremony location and the layout for the event. In addition to offering one more opportunity to build rapport with your clients, you'll get to meet the on-site coordinator who can instruct you on where the facility will allow you to set up your camera or cameras. By the way, most photographers never attend the rehearsal, so you may be able to use this opportunity to get an advantage over them when it comes to getting your camera positions and building rapport with the coordinator. Be very pleasant and helpful with everyone you meet.

Meeting the Ceremony Coordinator

You'll want to arrive about 15 minutes before the rehearsal begins in order to introduce yourself. When you introduce yourself to the coordinator, be respectful and treat him or her very well. This person may hold the key to the success of your shoot. I've been able to convince a coordinator to move flowers or people, and sometimes to allow *me* to move in order to get the best shot possible during particular moments of the ceremony. Very few videographers are successful at this.

Surveying the Location and Determining Camera Positions

For most weddings, whether indoor or outdoor, the two most common camera positions are referred to as the front camera and the back camera, as this indicates their location relative to the guests. The back camera is usually placed at the back of the church or behind the last row of pews or chairs that will be used by the guests (see Figure 8-1). Whenever possible, it should be placed in the aisle to center the shot. Two things you have to be aware of: You have to stay out of the aisle until after the wedding party and bride have made their walks down the aisle so you won't be in their way, and you have to be conscious of where the photographer sets up, as they will want to use the aisle also. In churches that have balconies in the back, I have preferred putting my second camera there since the view of the entire ceremony is usually not obstructed by anyone or any-

NOTE: If you're sitting facing the front of the church (altar), the groom's side will be on the right, the bride on the left. Jewish weddings are the opposite.

thing and most photographers prefer to shoot from downstairs at the back of the aisle.

The front camera should be positioned up front, on the groom's side facing the bride to capture the best shots of the bride during the ceremony (see Figure 8-1). Most churches will not allow you to set up on the altar area, but they should have a place for you off to the side of it. Make sure you can see the bride from there.

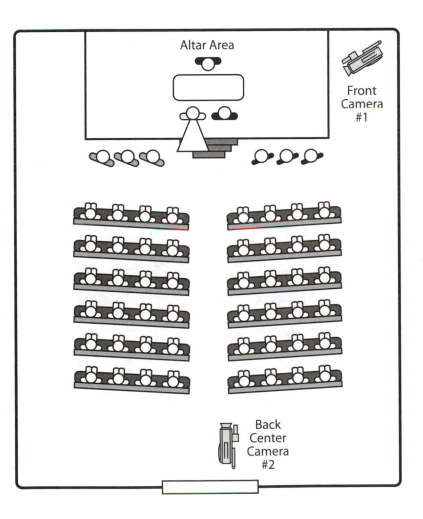

Figure 8-1
Two-camera set up.

If you decide to have a third camera, it could be placed almost anywhere, subject to the coordinator's approval. The most common location is at the front of the church, on the bride's side, on the opposite side of the altar as the front camera. See Figure 8-2 for possible locations.

As you watch the rehearsal process, stand in the locations permitted for your cameras so you'll be able to see what shots you'll be able to get during the ceremony. Pay attention to where the bride and groom will be positioned during most of the ceremony. Will they be facing the altar or the audience during most of the ceremony? This piece of information may be crucial when deter-

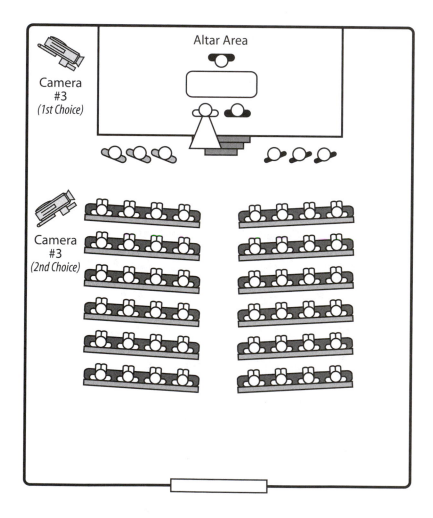

Figure 8-2
Possible locations for third camera.

mining your camera positions. Also, notice where and when they line up the groomsmen. After they are in position, can you still see the bride and groom? Do they block your view of the bride when she walks down the aisle? If so, there are a few possibilities to remedy this.

· Try to find a better position that falls within the church guidelines or is acceptable to the coordinator.

· Wait for a break in the rehearsal, when the coordinator is not talking to or working with anyone, then ask him or her if it would be possible to put some space between each groomsman so you'll be able to see the bride for at least part of the processional. Or ask the groomsmen if they can leave some space in between them and the person next to them.

· Ask the coordinator if you can move to a better position for the processional only, and let her know you'll move back to the designated position when the bride approaches the altar.

· If none of the previous three methods are successful, speak with the bride and groom and let them know that your view will be obstructed during certain portions (tell them which parts) of the ceremony. At this point, they will be aware of the problem and will have been informed that you cannot be held responsible for missed shots. Often, they can act as your ally in convincing the coordinator to help you find a solution. I recommend attempting to find a solution on your own before pursuing this option.

Remember, your clients expect *you* to be the professional and they will defer to your judgment on what makes a good video. This means don't ask your clients where they want you to set up. That's a big flag indicating that you may not be as professional as you have lead them to believe. You'll need to solve most of your videotaping problems on your own. That's why they hired you; *you're* supposed to be the professional.

When to Get the Client's Input

There will be times when you'll want to get the client's input. During one of my events, the church's minister would not allow me to move a tree which was blocking my shot to the back of the altar. I was forced to approach the client and inform them that they have two choices. I can try to shoot through the tree, in which case you'll see the branches in the shot, or I can shoot from the bride's side but I won't have a good shot of the bride's face during the vows. The client made the decision and therefore, knew what to expect in the final video. I was off the hook.

Getting Permission to Put a Mic on the Minister

If the minister (or clergy) is not present at the rehearsal you may want to ask the coordinator if the minister would be willing to wear a mic. The coordinator will either say sure, or they'll tell you to ask the minister before the ceremony.

If the minister is present at the rehearsal, introduce yourself as the videographer. Otherwise, you'll have to wait until before the ceremony to introduce yourself. Remember to be nice and respectful and ask him or her if it would be okay for you to put a wireless microphone on them for the actual ceremony on the wedding day. They will most likely respond in one of four ways.

1. "Yes, you may." This usually means they are familiar with the process and have no objection to it.

2. "Will your mic interfere with the church sound system?" Inform him or her that you will confirm that there will be no interference before you put a mic on him or her. Then, make sure you verify that there won't be any interference problem. This will be covered in the next chapter.

3. "I will already be wearing a mic." At this time, you will want to let them know that your mic is for the video recording only. If they still hesitate, refer to the reply for number 4.

4. "No." Inform them that your mic is for the video recording. Tell him or her that the couple feels that what he or she has to say during the ceremony is really important to them and they would really like it if he or she would wear a mic so, that it would be recorded for them to have indefinitely. This is a hard request to deny.

Once, I had a minister who responded, "I don't need to wear a mic; I project very well." There will be times when you'll just have to go without the minister's mic. Whatever you do, don't upset the minister! You won't like the consequences. If this is the case, then you may consider putting it on the altar table or the bride and groom's kneelers, if their ceremony utilizes one. This becomes valuable as a backup mic.

I cannot stress enough how important it is to be pleasant with every vendor you will work with throughout the wedding. I've heard numerous stories from other videographers about how many difficult photographers they've had to deal with. I, on the other hand, have had very few bad encounters. Some may say I'm just lucky, but I feel it's because I treat everyone the way I would like to be treated. When other vendors see that I act professionally and am courteous and helpful, they tend to extend the same courtesies back to me. It makes the wedding day go *much* easier.

Locating Additional Microphone Locations

If you're planning on putting a mic in front of the singer or musicians, ask the coordinator where they will be setting up. It's helpful to know where to look. Sometimes they may not show up until almost the last few moments before the ceremony. If you're planning on putting a mic on the podium to record the scripture readings, verify with the coordinator which podium will be used since many churches have one on both sides of the altar. The middle of the ceremony is not the time to find out you mic'd the wrong podium. During some rehearsals, the coordinator may have the readers practice a portion of the readings. Take note of which podium they approach, and then you won't need to ask the coordinator. For more information on how to set up the mics for these positions, see Chapter 9.

Additional Items to Consider

Throughout the rehearsal, note where the couple is instructed to walk. For example, when they approach the unity candle, do they approach from the left or the right side of the altar? It will be helpful to know whether your camera will be in their way or if you'll be able to get the shot. Some services have the couple present flowers to their parents. Catholic services have the bride offer flowers to the Virgin Mary. Pay attention to all of these movements and plan out how you want to capture them. If you're using two or more cameras, determine in advance which camera is responsible for taping each portion of the service. Refer to Chapter 9 for assistance in determining this. Make sure your other camera operators know which shots they are responsible for getting.

Final Suggestions Before You Leave

When you are ready to leave the rehearsal, be sure to say goodbye to your clients and reassure them that everything will be just fine. Also, don't forget to ask the coordinator what time the church will be available (on the day of the wedding) for you to set up your equipment. I recommend saying goodbye to the coordinator as well. The more chances you have to speak with them and show them how easy you are to work with, the more favors they'll be willing to do for you in the future.

Preparing for the Wedding Day

Since most rehearsals occur the day before the wedding, this is a good time to go over the preparations you need to make to be ready for the wedding day. I prefer to get all of my equipment together and packed up the day before the wedding so I can just get in my vehicle and go. This really comes in handy for when I have a wedding in the morning.

Make a Checklist

I strongly encourage you to create and consistently use a checklist for packing up your equipment. Sit down a make a list of all of the items you'll need for the wedding day shoot. This list should include but not be limited to the following:

- Camera
- Tripod
- Tripod dolly (if applicable)
- Fully charged camera batteries
- Blank tapes for all cameras
- Camera light (and battery belt, if applicable)
- Power cord for the camera (in case your batteries fail prematurely)
- Extension cords
- Microphones (both handheld and wireless) and cables
- Any other batteries needed for wireless mics or other equipment
- All of your adapters
- Backup equipment

Once you've completed your list, make sure there are checkboxes next to each item so you'll be able to check off each one as you pack it in your bag or vehicle. Put a couple of lines at the top of the form that ask for date and some kind of name identifier to identify the shoot, such as the name of the couple. Then make copies of it and fill one out for every shoot. This checklist may prove to be a lifesaver.

After everything has been packed into your bags, you may want to load up your vehicle. However, if your vehicle is going to be parked outside where anyone could break into it, then I'd suggest waiting until the morning of the wedding before you load it up. Also, make sure your vehicle has plenty of gas.

You should now be ready for the wedding day.

Chapter 9

Wedding Day, Pre-Ceremony

The wedding day is finally here, and now it's time to head out. Before you go, there are few more things you need to do.

Before You Leave Home

Make sure you are dressed appropriately. Here are a few guidelines to follow.

For Women

You should wear something nice and professional-looking like a blouse and slacks. Make sure your clothing will allow for you to move around freely. You'll have your arm raised in the air several times throughout the day so, your blouse will have to accommodate this. Don't wear tight-fitting slacks as you may frequently find yourself squatting down at different times throughout the day. If you're planning on operating the front camera, you may want to wear darker clothes so you'll blend in with the groomsmen better and not stand out too much. And finally, you'll want to wear comfortable shoes (*no heels!*) as you'll be on your feet most of the day. I would suggest rubber-soled shoes as they're quieter when you walk around the church.

For Men

You should wear something nice and professional-looking like a dark suit. Make sure your clothing will allow for you to move around freely. You'll have your arm raised in the air several times throughout the day so, your shirt will have to accommodate this. Don't wear tight-fitting pants as you may frequently find yourself squatting down at different times throughout the day. If you're planning on operating the front camera, you should wear dark clothes so you'll blend in with the groomsmen better and not stand out too much. And finally, you'll want to wear comfortable shoes as you'll be on your feet most of the day. I would suggest rubber-soled shoes as they're quieter when you walk around the church.

Items to Take with You

Make sure to put the questionnaire in your pocket where you can easily access it so you'll be able to refer to it throughout the day. You may want to take a bottle of water with you as you may get dehydrated during the day. It could really come in handy at the church or ceremony site where there may not be anything to drink on the premises. Sometimes I will even take a PowerBar or something to snack on in case I get hungry before I get a chance to eat at the reception. Keep in mind that shooting on the wedding day is very physically demanding. You'll be hauling around equipment and holding the camera for most of the day.

Don't Forget to Log Your Mileage

You need to have a mileage log in your vehicle at all times. The IRS allows you to deduct mileage for use of your vehicle. (Consult your tax advisor for more information on this.) Before you leave, write down the current date and the reason for the shoot. Then write down the odometer reading on your vehicle. When you get back from the shoot, write down the new odometer reading, then subtract your earlier reading from this one to get the total mileage traveled for the day. You should track this information for every shoot you go on. If you go to the client's place for consultations, log that mileage as well.

You'll also need to record your vehicle's odometer reading at the beginning and end of every year. This is used to determine how much of your total miles were used just for business. (Your tax preparer may need this information also.) You can purchase a mileage log at any office supply store.

Now it's time to go.

Arriving at the Ceremony Site

I recommend arriving at the ceremony location at least 90 minutes before the ceremony starts. If your client has scheduled you to begin taping prior to the ceremony then you should arrive at least 60 minutes before the time your client wants you to begin. You will need this time to get some location and establishing shots and for setting up your equipment. The following tasks are listed in no particular order. Since each wedding is different, the order you perform each of these may change from one wedding to another.

Greeting the Coordinator

When you arrive at the church, be sure to greet the ceremony coordinator you met at the rehearsal. If there's anyone else working in the church helping to set up, you may want to introduce yourself to them as well. Be polite and helpful whenever possible to anyone involved with preparations for the ceremony.

Setting Up Your Equipment

If the church (or ceremony location) is available when you arrive, you should be able to begin setting up your equipment right away.

Handling Potential Visual Obstacles

Usually about the same time you're setting up your equipment, there may be a florist setting up the flowers for the ceremony. You'll need to pay attention to where they put the large floral arrangements. I've had a few weddings where the florist put a tall arrangement right between my camera and the aisle, totally blocking any shot I might have of the bride's entrance.

In one instance, knowing how important this shot is, I spoke with the church coordinator to see if there was another place the flowers could be placed and still be seen. As it turns out, the coordinator didn't like where the flowers were placed either, so she had the florist move the flowers toward the back of the altar area where the church normally displays flowers arrangements. It sure paid off getting to know the coordinator at the rehearsal. I would've had a very difficult time explaining to the bride why I didn't get a good shot of her and her dad walking down the aisle.

Outdoor weddings may have a gazebo or an archway at the front of the aisle instead of an altar area. If an archway is used, the minister will stand beneath it. If a gazebo is used, the minister and sometimes the couple will be inside of it. Both of these items may cause an obstruction of your view, so be careful where you place your camera for these weddings. For example, an archway may not have enough room between one side of it and the minister for you to try to shoot between them. In these cases, I'll try to shoot between the archway and the best man. Sometimes I may have to nudge the best man out of the way to clear a path.

If any objects are going to be placed in your way, keeping you from getting the important shots, this is a good time to see if there's another way around it. You may have to move your camera to a different position. Unfortunately, in most cases, these objects are not set up at the time of the rehearsal.

Microphone Placement

For the weddings I shoot, I use up to four separate microphones. I'll put one on the groom, the minister, the reader's podium, and the soloist or musicians. If I had to use wired mics for all of these, then I would have cables running all over the church. I would either have to tape down all of the cables or risk someone tripping over them. This is the main reason I prefer to use wireless mics. I will then connect all of my mics to an audio mixer (mentioned in Chapter 3) and control all four mics from here. If there won't be any readings, then I'll skip the reader's podium. If there's no soloist or musicians besides the organist, then I'll skip that one as well. You don't need a mic for the organist as you'll hear the organ from everywhere in the church.

As you are starting out, you may want to only use two mics, one for the groom and one for the minister. Depending on your camera, you should be able to connect each mic to each mic input on your camera. If you are shooting with two cameras, you could connect one mic to each camera. This will leave your camera's second audio channel open for recording the ambient sound.

If you are brave, and depending on the cameras being used, you could try connecting the groom and the minister's mics to one camera and connect the podium and soloist mics to the other camera. You can also use a portable recorder, like a minidisk recorder, with a mic if you need to.

You should test every wireless microphone that you intend to use for the ceremony to make sure there won't be any interference problems. Make sure all of the wireless mics have fresh batteries in both the transmitter and receiver. When I've finished testing my mics, I'll put a wireless lav on the reader podium by wrapping the mic cord around the gooseneck mic that's attached to the podium. I'll then put the transmitter somewhere on the side or inside the podium (if possible) so that it's out of the reader's way. Turn off this transmitter until 10 to 20 minutes before the ceremony to save the battery. Don't forget to turn off the receiver as well.

If there's going to be a soloist, I will put a mic next to the church's mic that the soloist will be using. If there's a musician instead of a soloist, I'll set a mic near them. If there's going to be both, then I'll place the mic by the soloist. I'm more interested in recording him or her than the musicians, and I know the mic will usually pick up the instruments as well. Turn off this transmitter and receiver also until 10 to 20 minutes before the ceremony to save the batteries.

I don't put a mic on the groom or the minister until about 15 minutes before the start of the ceremony. Often, you'll find the groom in the same part of the church as the minister, and they'll often walk out to the altar together at the beginning of the ceremony. If you only have two mics, then don't worry about the readings or soloist.

Additional Sources of Sound

Some videographers like to plug into the church's sound system. If you know how to do this, I'd recommend hooking this source into only your back camera and attaching the receivers from the groom's mic and minister's mic into your front camera. If you don't know how to plug into the sound system, then I strongly encourage you to avoid trying it.

What to Videotape Before the Ceremony

Make sure you have a tape in your camera. If your camera has the ability to record color bars, I recommend doing so. Check the camera's instruction manual to determine if this feature is available and how to activate it. Record at least 15 seconds of color bars. I will usually turn off the color bars and

Figure 9-1
Front of a church.

record for another 15 seconds with the lens cap on. This is one method for recording some black on your tape. The other method is to close the iris all of the way. It's always good to have some black at the beginning of your tape. Now, record something for about five to 10 seconds and then play it back to ensure your camera is operating properly. If everything is functioning properly then, you're ready to begin.

Establishing Shots

At every wedding, I will get a few shots of the front of the church (see Figure 9-1. Sometimes I will have to go across the street in order to get the entire front of the church in the shot. Once I've finished getting all of my outside shots, I'll try to get various creative shots inside the church, including the flower arrangements. For outdoor weddings, you should get shots of the location and the whole setup, including flowers, archways, and decorations. I have often used some of these shots at the beginning of my videos and many times as a backdrop for when I scroll the wedding invitation across the screen. If time permits, I may try to get shots of the limo as well.

Figure 9-2
Front of another church.

Bride and Groom Getting Ready

Depending on when the bride wants you to begin taping and if there's enough time, I recommend trying to get some shots of the bride getting ready. Most churches have a bridal room for the bride and bridesmaids to finish getting ready for the ceremony. If you can, go into this room and get some shots of the bride and bridesmaids putting on makeup, putting jewelry on the bride, or any other preparation activities.

You may also try to get some shots of the groom and groomsmen's final preparations. You may find them in a separate room or roaming around the church somewhere.

During these final preparations may be a good time to ask the bride and groom if they want to record a personal message to each other before the ceremony. Sometimes, I'll discuss this with them during the original consultation and get their approval at that time. In case I didn't, I'll ask them at the wedding. The idea is to not let the other person see the special message until the couple watches their final edited video. It makes for a great surprise.

Guest Arrivals

Videotaping the guests arriving is another way to make the wedding video more interesting. Capture them as they walk up to the church, while they are visiting with other guests, when they enter the building, or signing the guest book (see Figure 9-3).

Pre-ceremony Photo Session

I always ask my clients if they want me to videotape their photo sessions with the photographer before the ceremony. Usually, the bride will have photos taken with her family and bridesmaids but without the groom. And the groom will have photos taken with his family and the groomsmen but without the bride. If my clients want me to record this then I'll shoot some footage of the photo session and also some footage of whatever else may be going on around the photo shoot.

Don't Forget About Your Other Camera Operators

Don't forget to give your other camera operators a blank tape to record with. If you have any last-minute instructions for them on what you want them to shoot, this is the time to let them know. For ideas on what to have them shoot, refer to Chapter 10.

Introduce Yourself to the Photographer

The first chance you get, introduce yourself to the photographer if he or she is not busy. Let them know you'll try your best to stay out of their way. Tell them to let you know if you happen to be in their shot. These types of comments will let them know that you're willing to work with them and they might prompt the photographer to try to stay out of *your* shots. The day will go a lot smoother if the two of you can get along with each other.

It doesn't hurt to introduce yourself to the limo driver or any other vendor you happen to run into throughout the day. You never know where your next referral might come from.

Introduce Yourself to the Minister

If you haven't already done so, you'll need to introduce yourself to the minister and make sure it's okay to put a mic on him or her. You need to do this no

Figure 9-3
Signing the guest book.

later than 15 minutes before the ceremony. If you encounter any problems getting the minister to wear your mic, refer to the steps listed in the section on Putting a Mic on the Minister in Chapter 8.

Be aware that the minister usually has several articles of clothing he or she has to put on, including a robe, so you may want to help him or her put your mic on. Some ministers may tell you that they will put the mic on themselves. This is fine, but just make sure the mic transmitter is already turned on. Tell them that the mic is on and they don't have to worry about turning it on or off as you'll be controlling that from your camera. Even if this is not necessarily true, you should tell them anyway as it will keep them from getting the urge to shut the mic off for any reason.

At one of my weddings, in the middle of the ceremony the minister decided to turn off his mic that was connected to the church's sound system so, he could talk to the couple in private. He not only turned off the church's mic, but he turned off mine, too. When he turned the church's mic back on, he forgot to turn my mic on. It stayed off for the rest of the ceremony.

Interacting with Guests

While you're videotaping the pre-ceremony activities and guests mingling, occasionally one or more of the guests may start talking to the camera, congratulating the couple. If this happens, continue videotaping them and let them finish. Your camera mic may actually pick up the words they are saying and you may want to use the footage in the final video, so be alert.

If you find yourself needing to speak with any of the guests for any reason, just be sure to be polite. Don't let any of the guests keep you from doing your job and missing something important.

Putting a Mic on the Groom

About 15 minutes before the ceremony, you'll need to put a microphone on the groom. If you haven't officially met the groom yet, go up to him and introduce yourself. Tell him you're going to put a mic on him to record the vows. If the groom is wearing a tuxedo or a suit, then you should attach the mic onto his lapel. Attach the belt pack transmitter to his belt or the waistline of his pants in the middle of his back. Then, make sure the entire cord between the mic and the transmitter is completely hidden under his tuxedo or suit jacket. If you have an extra-long cable, then you may want to wrap some of the excess cable around the belt clip of the transmitter until the cable is completely hidden beneath the jacket.

If the groom isn't wearing a tuxedo or suit, then you'll still attach the transmitter to his belt or waistband of his pants. You'll have to attach the mic to the front of his shirt. If the shirt has buttons then you may want to attach the mic near the buttons. The mic cord should be hidden under his shirt, so that only the mic is visible.

After I've finished putting the mic on the groom and I have made sure the mic is turned on, I'll tell the groom that the mic is on and not to touch it. Some grooms may be nervous that I might accidentally record an inappropriate or private comment from them before the ceremony. To put a groom at ease, I'll let him know that I won't be recording anything he says until after the ceremony has begun.

Years ago, I hired someone else to videotape one of my weddings. After the videographer had put the mic on the groom, he left the room. The groom then decided to turn off the mic to make sure that what he was about to say would not be recorded. Unfortunately, the videographer at this wedding was only using one mic besides the camera mic, and the groom never turned that mic back on. The only audio we had of the entire ceremony was from the camera mic. We had to do some real creative editing for the vows in this video.

Final Check Before the Ceremony

Make sure you've turned the podium and soloist mics back on. Be sure to turn on all of the wireless receivers as well. Now that all of the mics are in position and turned on, use your headphones to verify that they are working properly. Make sure all of your camera operators are in place and ready to start taping. It's time to begin taping the ceremony.

Chapter 10
Taping the Ceremony

Now that everything is working properly and all camera operators are in position, it's time for the ceremony to begin. At most weddings, there is usually music playing while the guests are being seated, so how do you know when the actual ceremony has started?

When to Begin Recording

There are two indicators to look for. The first clue to look for is when the grandparents are being escorted down the aisle to their seats. Be ready to start recording as you don't want to miss this. I consider this to be the beginning of the ceremony, so I'll continue recording until the end of the service.

If there are no grandparents, then look for the parents waiting at the back of the church as they prepare to walk down the aisle. A new song will start, and the parents will begin walking (see Figure 10-1). This is the time to start taping as this marks the beginning of the ceremony. Again, continue recording until the ceremony has ended.

Handling the Audio

In Chapter 9, I mentioned that you need to make sure all of your microphone transmitters and receivers are turned on and functioning properly before the ceremony starts. I recommend plugging headphones into your cameras in order to

Figure 10-1
Seating of the
parents.

monitor the sound you are receiving from the mics. For each camera you are using, make sure your audio recording levels are set properly in your camera if your camera has the ability to do so. If you're not sure how to set the audio levels, consult the instruction manual. For more information and tips on audio equipment, how to operate, and solving audio challenges, visit for audio-related training products.

Camera Moving

In most churches, they usually don't allow you to move with your camera after the ceremony has begun. During the ceremony, there may be times when you may want to try to move the front camera a few feet in one direction or an-

Figure 10-2
Bride's entrance.
Some weddings will
have the mother
accompany the bride
down the aisle in
addition to the father.

other in the attempt to get a better shot of some of the activities. If you have
to move, try not to draw attention to yourself during the process.

The Processional

The processional consists of the portion of the ceremony beginning with the
seating of the grandparents and parents and continues until the bride has
completed her walk down the aisle and is positioned next to the groom, just
before the minister begins to address the audience.

The typical processional will include the entrance of the minister, groom,
groomsmen, bridesmaids, ring bearer, flower girl or girls, maid of honor, and
the bride (see Figure 10-2). Some weddings may include the entrance of a coin
bearer, Bible bearer, junior bridesmaids and junior groomsmen, and sponsors.

Various religions and cultures may include variations of the above and may include other people, so you may want to ask your client who will be involved in the processional.

Front Camera Shots

The front camera will usually have the best position for filming this portion of the ceremony, since the wedding party will be walking towards it. It's crucial to have your camera on a tripod during this segment if possible. You may want to zoom in towards the back of the aisle and frame and focus on the first set of people who come down the aisle. Then, zoom out as they proceed down the aisle. If the next group of people are close behind the first group, then you should leave your camera in the wide-angle setting. Don't zoom in again unless there is a large gap between groups. When the bride enters, try to zoom in and follow her with her father (or escort, if applicable) all of the way down the aisle, zooming out as they get closer to you. Be sure to stay zoomed in close enough to get a good shot of the bride's father handing her off to the groom; there are often some special moments that can be captured at this time. In the final edit of the video, most of the footage you'll be using will be from this camera during this segment.

BONUS TIP: In some churches, we've been allowed to move our front camera near the altar or at the front of the aisle only during the processional to get better shots. I'll use my tripod dolly to roll the camera out towards the aisle for taping the processional. Once the bride gets to the front of the aisle, I'll roll back to my designated position for the ceremony. The dolly keeps the shot fairly smooth while I'm moving the camera. Ask the coordinator about this before you try it. If you just do it without their permission, they may not let you shoot there again.

Back Camera Shots

Whenever possible, the back camera should also be on a tripod. This camera's position will only allow you to see the backs of the members of the wedding party as they walk away from you. This camera should start recording at the same time the first camera starts and continue taping throughout the entire ceremony. This will allow you to easily synchronize both cameras during the editing process. Even though this camera will only be recording the backs of people's heads, these shots may become critical for using as cutaways for the front camera during zooming or repositioning for the next shot. Be sure to zoom in when there are little kids walking down the aisle; they tend to provide some of the most interesting footage.

The most critical shots for this camera to get during the processional are the groom's reaction when he sees the bride coming down the aisle and the shot of the bride's entire backside and her train as this will provide the best shot of the back of the wedding dress, the view the bride will never have as long as she is wearing the dress. Brides *love* this footage as they probably spent a lot of time choosing the dress. So, be careful in getting a good mix of these two shots since, they happen around the same time. You should follow the bride (zooming in) up to the altar to get the shot of the bride's father handing her off to the groom. Remain zoomed in for a little while to allow time for the front camera to get repositioned, if necessary.

> **Please Note:** Third camera shots will not be covered in this book.

Opening Remarks

After the bride has reached the altar, most ceremonies will continue with the minister's opening comments (see Figure 10-3). At this time, he or she may ask, "Who gives this woman to be married to this man?" The bride's father and sometimes the whole family will respond, "I do" or "We do." After this, the minister will often tell the congregation to be seated. During some ceremonies you'll see the bride and groom kneel down on kneelers.

Front Camera Shots

The front camera should stay zoomed in on the couple and the bride's father while he is still standing next to them. Try to get a good shot of Dad answering the minister's question. When Dad goes to sit down, don't worry about following him; remain focused on the couple.

Back Camera Shots

The back camera should also stay zoomed in on the couple and Dad, along with the minister, since he will be the one talking at this time. Once everyone has started to sit down, you may want to start zooming out to a wider shot to prepare for the reader in case they have one.

Figure 10-3
Minister giving his
opening remarks.

Scripture Readings

After the minister has finished his or her opening remarks, asked the question, and instructed the guests to sit down, he or she or someone from the audience will go to the podium to read a scripture. Some ceremonies may have two or three of them read by as many as three different people. When there's more than one person reading, they will often go to the podium one at a time.

Front Camera Shots

The front camera is usually positioned in such a way that you can see only the back of the readers. During the readings, zoom in on the couple. You may also be able to get some shots of the wedding party, parents, family, and guests at this time, if you can see them from where you are. Try to keep your camera still for at least 10 to 15 seconds before attempting to move to a different shot.

Back Camera Shots

The back camera should zoom in on the readers during the readings as this camera will have the best view of them (see Figure 10-4). Keep in mind that many couples will choose people who are special to them to do these readings so, it is just as important to tape them as the wedding party. You may want to zoom out when they finish and start walking back to their seats. This will allow your shot to include the couple as well as the next reader approaching the altar.

Sermons

After the readings or instead of them, the minister will give his or her sermon.

Front Camera Shots

The front camera is usually positioned in such a way that you can see only the back of the minister at this time. Continue with close-ups of the couple and shots of the audience if you can. I will usually get several shots of different small groups of people that I can use as cutaway shots later.

Figure 10-4
Reader.

Figure 10-5
Sermon.

Back Camera Shots

The back camera should zoom in on the minister during the sermon as this provides the best shot of him or her (see Figure 10-5). You may want to use a variety of shots during this time, including close-ups of the minister, medium shots of the minister and the couple, and some wide shots of the whole church. Make sure to stay with the same shot for a minimum of 30 seconds before changing the zoom or composition of your shot. This will allow for easier editing when mixing the two cameras.

I always tell the person operating the back camera to shoot as if they are the *only* camera. This means that when you zoom in or out, do it smoothly. This should ensure that you'll always have a usable shot during the editing process.

Vows and Ring Exchange

At some point, after the sermon, the minister will ask the couple to turn and face each other. It's time for the vows. After the vows, they'll proceed to the exchange of rings. Most ceremonies will have the groom go first.

Front Camera Shots

Normally, the front camera should be able to see most of the bride's face but only a slight profile of the groom from behind. During the vows, zoom in on both of their faces (see Figure 10-6). You should be able to see both of them in the shot. You may choose to zoom in closer on the bride during her vows. For the ring exchange, I recommend pulling out to a medium shot where you can see their faces and their hands.

Back Camera Shots

Typically, the back camera will only be able to zoom in to a medium, head-to-waist shot (see Figure 10-7). This is due to the distance the camera will be from the couple. That's fine. If you're able to zoom in closer than the previously mentioned medium shot, try to focus on the faces for the vows and return to the medium shot for the ring exchange so you'll be able to see their hands and faces (see Figure 10-8). Since the front camera can't see the groom very well, it will be up to the back camera to focus on the groom when he speaks.

Figure 10-6
Vows, Front Camera.

Figure 10-7
Vows, Back Camera.

Unity Candle

Most ceremonies will have a ritual signifying two lives becoming one. The most common ritual involves the lighting of a unity candle (see Figure 10-9). For some ceremonies they may choose to pour two separate vases of sand into a third vase at the same time or some other similar ritual in place of the lighting of the unity candle. Regardless of which version they use, the videotaping process is the same. The couple will usually have to walk over to the props, perform the ritual, and walk back to their original places. In some weddings they will approach their parents to present them with flowers before they return to their original places; so be ready.

There may also be someone singing at this time. Be sure to focus on the couple first while they light the candle. After the couple has returned to their original location and if the person is still singing, whichever camera has a better shot should zoom in on the singer. The other camera should stay with the couple. Be aware that sometimes the couple may stay standing by the unity candle until the singer finishes the song. If this happens, then whichever camera has the better shot of the singer should zoom in on that person.

Figure 10-8
Rings.

Figure 10-9
Unity candle.

Front Camera Shots

The front camera may or may not have a good shot of the lighting of the unity candle. If you do, then get the couple's faces, hands, and the unity candle in the shot (a head-to-waist shot). This is an important shot. Then follow them back to their original places.

Back Camera Shots

The back camera should follow the couple to the unity candle and maintain a head-to-waist shot during the lighting of the candle (see Figure 10-10) whenever possible. Then follow the couple back to their places. If the couple presents flowers to their parents, be sure to follow them and get this shot—it's an important one.

Soloist and Singers

Many ceremonies may feature a soloist or singing duo for one or more songs during the ceremony. If there is nothing else happening while they are singing,

Figure 10-10
Lighting the unity candle.

then the camera with the best shot should zoom in on the singer or singers. The other camera should focus on the couple.

Other Activities to Watch For

Depending on the religion or cultural customs, there may be additional ceremonial activities added to the wedding ceremony. Here are just a few of the more common ones.

Catholic Mass (Communion)

Most ceremonies in the Catholic faith are part of a Mass, which includes the Eucharist, or Communion. It begins with a series of sermon-like rituals performed by the priest while preparing the bread and wine. The back camera offers the best view of this. The front camera can continue getting shots of the couple, wedding party, and guests. The priest will then give the bread to the couple along with a drink of wine. He will then proceed to offer the bread to the rest of the wedding party, family, and the rest of the congregation. The front camera will have the best shot of this. I will usually stop taping when they have finished with the wedding party and family. I will resume after the communion is over and the priest is ready to say a final prayer or blessing. I have found that most couples don't want to see the rest of their guests receiving communion.

Coin or Bible Ceremony

Some cultures include a ritual known as the coin ceremony. A bag of coins is placed in the groom's hands, and he gives them to the bride. I have done a wedding or two where a Bible was also exchanged in a similar fashion. Shoot these the same as the vows and rings. The front camera should have the better view.

Cord or Lasso and Veil

Some cultures include a ritual known as the cord and veil or the lasso and veil. This is where a couple of sponsors will place a veil over the couple's backs (see Figure 10-11). Then another couple of sponsors will place a rope (referred to as the cord or lasso) over the couple's shoulders (see Figure 10-12). Shoot this

Figure 10-11
Veil ritual.

the same as the ring exchange. The front camera should have the better view. Be sure to include the sponsors in the shot.

Flowers to Mary

The Catholic religion includes a ritual involving placing flowers at the feet of a statue of the Virgin Mary. Have both cameras follow the couple for this.

Jewish Weddings

Jewish weddings have several rituals unique to their religion. You may want to research these more. Here is a list of some activities to watch for:

- The signing of the ketubah.
- Weddings are performed in a synagogue instead of a church, or at another location.
- The groom walks down the aisle with his parents, as does the bride.
- Be aware that the bride and groom will stand on the opposite sides from other ceremonies.
- A rabbi presides over the ceremony instead of a minister.

Figure 10-12
Cord or lasso ritual.

- The bride, groom, both sets of parents, the rabbi, and sometimes others will all be standing under a canopy referred to as the chuppa.
- The groom will break a glass with his foot just before the kiss.

These are just some of the traditions to look for. For more information about Jewish weddings, go to www.theknot.com/ch_article.html?Object=AI990319162144

The Kiss, Pronouncement, and Recessional

After most of the rituals have been completed, it will be time for the kiss. Both cameras should zoom in for this as you never know which way the couple will turn during their kiss (see Figure 10-13). It's good to have two angles to choose from in the editing process.

After the kiss, at the end of the service, the couple will turn and face the audience as the minister pronounces them as husband and wife or some variation of that, and the couple will then proceed back up the aisle followed by the rest of the wedding party.

Figure 10-13
The kiss.

The recessional is similar to the processional but in reverse. The back camera will now become the primary camera for getting this segment as the wedding party will be walking towards that camera. The back camera, after having zoomed in for the kiss, should follow the couple while zooming out until they have walked out of your shot. Then keep a medium shot as the rest of the wedding party walks in and out of your shot. The front camera should continue recording for cover shots or cutaways as needed for the back camera.

I will keep recording until all of the wedding party and family members have passed by my back camera. Now that the ceremony is over, it's time for the post-ceremony coverage.

Outdoor Weddings

Outdoor weddings (see Figure 10-14) are similar to the church weddings I've just described in terms of how they should be shot. There won't be as many rituals as the church weddings, though.

Special Situation to Watch For

Always try to confirm in advance which direction the couple will be facing during most of the ceremony. In some weddings, the couple faces the audience. If this is the case, the back camera will now have a better view than the front camera. The front camera will still need to be in front for the processional, but it may need to be moved to the outside of the audience on the groom's side (see Figure 10-15) or somewhere else.

After the Ceremony

At most weddings, there's usually about 10 minutes from the time the wedding party leaves the church until the photographer gets set up and the wedding party has returned to the altar area for portraits (often referred to as "formals"). During this time, you may want to recover your microphones from wherever you've placed them and start packing up your gear. You'll need to be ready to leave right after the photo session. It helps to have an assistant to help you pack up so you don't miss any of the post-ceremony coverage. You should

Figure 10-14
Typical outdoor wedding setup.

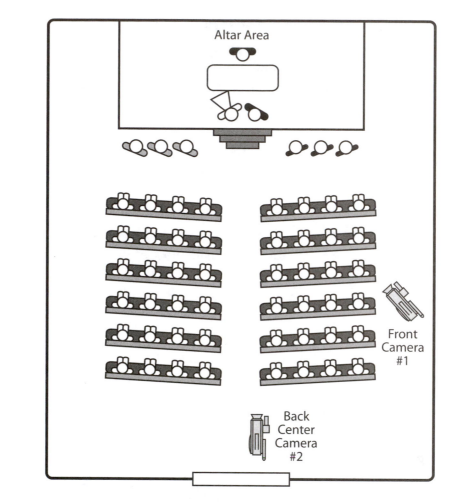

Figure 10-15
Alternate location for
front camera.

need to keep out only your camera, camera battery, and maybe a light or tri-pod. I do most of my post-ceremony taping without a tripod, which means holding the camera a lot.

Taping the Photo Session

Many videographers will stand next to the photographer (being careful to stay out of his or her way) and videotape the people as they pose for the photos (see Figure 10-16). If you choose to do this, try to find ways to make your shots more creative than the photographer's shots; don't just duplicate the still photos. For example, you may want to put your camera near the ground and get a low-angle shot. For large groups, you may want to pan the crowd by zooming in and starting from one side, then pan across to the other side. Don't forget, video is considered a close-up medium, meaning that you need to focus more on people's faces and less on shots from far away.

Make your video more interesting by shooting the people who are watching the photos being taken (the spectators). Be sure to get some video of the kids; they usually provide some entertaining moments. Behind-the-scenes shots can be useful, as well. Be creative.

Posing the Couple

Many videographers like to get some footage of their own with the couple. In order to do this, you'll want to make arrangements with the couple beforehand to allow you some time to shoot some special footage after the photographer has finished the portraits. You should already have planned what you're going to do with them or at least have some ideas. This will make your time with them go smoothly and you'll look more like a professional. The

Figure 10-16
Photo session.

Figure 10-17
Limo departing.

bride and groom have put their trust in you, so you'll be able to direct them by telling them what you want them to do. Be sure you have them doing things that involve movement and interaction, not just posing.

Taping the Limo Departure

You may want to tape the couple getting into the limo and maybe have them toast each other or give each other a kiss inside the limo. One of my favorite shots is to get in front of the limo, on the sidewalk at a low angle, and shoot the limo coming towards me and driving out of the shot (see Figure 10-17). Then, I'll spin around to get the limo from behind as it pulls away. It's a great shot for fading to black.

Additional Footage

If time permits, you may want to get some additional shots of the location, flowers, or anything you think may be useful or relevant. If you don't have time, don't worry about it.

Packing Up

If you haven't already finished packing up your equipment, now is the time. Make sure you have everything you came with.

Thanking the Church Staff

I recommend thanking the church coordinator and minister for all of their help, even if they weren't that much help. It helps build trust that may be beneficial in the future. It could lead to referrals or special favors at a later date.

Chapter 11
The Reception

Now that the ceremony part of the day is over, it's time to redirect our attention to preparing for and recording the reception. Let's start by determining the equipment you'll need for rest of the wedding day.

Equipment Needed

You should have the following items with you for the reception: camera; fully charged batteries for the camera; camera light; handheld microphone (wired or wireless); a pair of headphones; plenty of blank tape; and a wireless lav mic with transmitter, receiver, and fresh batteries.

Connecting with the DJ or Band

You should have already found out from your client whether they will be having a DJ or a band entertain their guests for the reception. Upon arriving at the reception site, try to locate the DJ (or the person in charge of the band's mixing board, if there is a band). When you find him or her, introduce yourself. It is very important to establish a good working relationship with them as soon as possible. While you're setting up your equipment, you may want to ask him or her if they could provide you with advanced notice before the key events are about to start. For the remainder of this discussion, I will use the term DJ to represent the DJ or the band's representative.

Methods of Acquiring Sound from the DJ or Band

I've found that it is crucial to record audio directly from the DJ or band's sound system for the wedding party introductions and the toasts. The quality of the sound acquired during these activities is one of the largest factors that separate an amateur from a professional. There are different methods for acquiring sound from a DJ or band. I'll discuss a few of them here. The following methods will require the use of a wireless microphone system. The receiver should be attached to your camera and contain fresh batteries. Go ahead and plug your headphones into your camera.

Placing a Mic on the Speaker

Take out your wireless lav mic like the one you placed on the groom for the ceremony. Place the transmitter on top of one of the main speakers that's connected to the DJ or band's sound system. Most of these speakers will have two or three drivers facing the front of the speaker. Let the lav mic dangle in front of the speaker with the microphone element placed directly in front of the smallest driver (see Figure 11-1). Use the weight of the transmitter to secure the microphone in the proper location by placing the transmitter on top of the excess cord. Turn on the transmitter and the receiver. Have the DJ play something through the speakers. Using your headphones, you should be able to confirm that your mic is working properly.

Pointing a Mic Towards a Speaker

You could put a shotgun mic on a mic stand and place it in front of the speaker with the mic pointed directly to one of the smaller speaker drivers. Be advised that in some cases, the speakers may be positioned right next to the dance floor, and if you put a mic stand in front of it, people may trip over the stand on the way to and from the dance floor.

Figure 11-1
Placing a mic on the
speaker.

Tapping Directly into the Sound Board

This method is really more of an advanced topic and involves the need for a better understanding of how audio equipment needs to be interconnected. I strongly recommend the audio workshop program provided by ProVideo Training as they show you everything you need to know about this process. For now, I'll just cover the basic concept.

In Chapter 3, I discussed different types of audio connectors, and this is where that information will really come in handy. Most DJs' sound boards will have RCA-style outputs, so you'll need a combination of an attenuator (to convert line level to mic level in order to avoid distortion of the sound) and special cables or adapters to convert from RCA connectors to the type of plug used with your wireless transmitter (where your mic plugs into).

If you have the proper equipment for making this connection, ask the DJ if they have an audio output from their mixing board that you can plug into. Don't be surprised if they don't understand what you're asking for. Tell them you need the audio feed so you'll be able to record the announcements and the toasts. There will be some DJs that may not be comfortable with this idea. At one wedding, I had a DJ tell me that the last time she let someone do this, they couldn't get her equipment to function properly.

Once you have received permission, you should give the DJ the end of your RCA cable and have him or her plug it into their board. Don't ever touch someone else's equipment without their permission. Finish connecting the other end to your transmitter and turn on the transmitter. Use your headphones to verify that you are receiving sound from the DJ.

Verify That Everything Works

After you have successfully connected your transmitter to the sound system, have the DJ test the microphone that will be used to announce the bridal party. It's very important to make sure that you can hear the DJ in order to record the bridal party introductions. At another wedding, I confirmed that everything was working fine and I could hear the DJ's music perfectly. When it came time to record the introductions, the music came through fine, but I couldn't hear the DJ introducing the wedding party. I discovered later that I was plugged into the wrong part of his mixing board and I wasn't receiving the full mix, which included the DJ's mic.

Secondary Sound Source

Your camera should have come with a microphone, either built-in or attached. You will use this mic to record all of the ambient sounds of the reception such as the laughter and applause from the guests as the evening unfolds. Most cameras have the ability to record two separate channels of audio, so you can use one of them for the ambient sound and the other for your feed from the DJ or band. Most cameras with a miniplug external mic jack will automatically shut off the camera mic when you plug in an external mic. If you have this kind of camera, then you'll need to purchase a small shotgun-style mic to attach to the top of the camera for recording the ambient sound. You'll also need a portable mixer. (Refer to Chapter 3 for information on audio mixers.) The external mic jack on most of these cameras is a stereo jack that will allow you to be able to send two distinct channels of audio (one into the left channel, the other into the right channel) using an audio mixer. The feed from the DJ or band will go to one channel, and the ambient sound from the mic you've attached to your camera will go to the other channel. The ambient mic is vital for capturing the sounds of the party.

Final Preparations

If you haven't already done so, attach your light to your camera. Make sure you have a fully charged battery on your camera and at least 30 minutes of blank tape left to record the bridal party entrance and possibly a toast or a first dance. I always check with the DJ or MC to find out if there will be any other activities happening after the wedding party introductions but before everyone sits down to eat. Put on your headphones. Make sure you can still hear the sound from the DJ's or band's sound system. Check your light to be sure it works. Record a few seconds of something, then play it back to confirm that your camera is recording properly. If everything seems to be functioning correctly, then you are ready to begin taping the reception.

Preliminary Shots

If you have time before the grand entrance, you should get some establishing shots of the reception location. For example, if it's being held in a hotel, you may want to get a shot of the front of the hotel. Shoot some footage of the room, preferably before any of the guests have entered. Make sure to get close-ups of the decorations, flowers, and anything else in the room that is unique to this wedding. And don't forget to get a shot of the wedding cake (see Figure 11-2. Then you may proceed to videotape the guests mingling during the cocktail hour. Some couples choose to have some additional photos taken on the grounds of the reception site; you may want to tape some of this as well. With all of this out of the way, it's time to start the reception.

The Grand Entrance

Most wedding receptions will begin with an introduction of the wedding party. The DJ or MC will read the names of the wedding party members, usually in pairs, as they enter the room or reception area. The best methods of determining which doorway they will enter from is to either ask the DJ (or MC) or find the doorway that the wedding party is lining up behind. You'll need to know this to ensure you'll be facing the appropriate entrance when you begin

Figure 11-2
Shot of the cake.

recording the introductions. You should be at least 20 feet from the entrance so you can record a significant portion of each couple's entrance. Whenever possible, try to find a spot near the pathway they will be walking through, so they will walk right by your camera.

Start taping the first couple being introduced by zooming in to a medium, head-to-waist shot. Smoothly zoom out as they approach you, and when they are a few feet away from you, let them walk out of the frame of your shot. After they've walked out of your shot, begin zooming in on the next couple. You'll discover that most DJs will announce the names of the next couple soon after the previous couple, so be ready. Keep the camera movements smooth as you'll probably be using the entire shot as is, without editing it.

At some weddings, in preparation for the announcement of the bride and groom, the staff may close the doors to the entrance immediately after the best man and maid of honor have entered the room. If this happens and the DJ tries to "pump up" the audience prior to announcing the couple, you may have an opportunity to shoot some cutaway footage of some of the guests at their tables. If there isn't enough time for this then, go ahead and zoom in on the bride and groom (or the doorway if the door is closed), and zoom out as they approach you (see Figure 11-3). This time you may want to continue following them as they pass your camera. I suggest following them all of the way to either the dance floor, if they are planning on going right to the first dance, or to their table. Keep the camera rolling until the applause has died down. If you know there's going to be a toast, a blessing, or some type of activity immediately after the introductions then, you may want to keep the camera rolling.

> **NOTE:** The order of the remaining reception activities will vary from wedding to wedding. The order I have them listed in is what I've found to be the order most often used.

What Happens Next?

After the grand entrance, any of the following may occur:

- The couple's first dance
- The toast
- The blessing of the meal
- Straight to serving the meal

Figure 11-3
Bride and groom's
entrance.

The Meal

If they proceed directly to serving the meal, then you may want to use this time to get some shots of the wedding cake and anything else you may not have been able to get yet. I will use this time to eat, so I'll be ready to begin taping when the activities resume.

If they do not go directly to the meal, then proceed to the appropriate section on how to cover the different activities.

The First Dance

During the first dance, most of the focus of your videotaping will be on the couple. I recommend shooting a combination of close-up shots, medium shots, and wide shots of the couple. Close-ups involve zooming in on their faces and capturing them interacting with each other either kissing to conversing. Don't worry about trying to record what they are saying; I try to avoid it. Medium shots are from head to waist (see Figure 11-4). Wide shots may include head to toe, especially when the bride's back is facing you. This will provide

Figure 11-4
First dance.

another great opportunity to capture the back of the bride's dress. A wide shot may also include the bride or groom's parents (in the background) along with the couple, as they watch them dance. This offers a nice vantage point that will allow me to smoothly zoom in on the parents in case I see an emotional moment developing.

As you vary your camera between these different types of shots, be sure to keep the movements as smooth as possible. This will save you many hours of editing later. When you're in a close-up or medium shot, be prepared to zoom out quickly should the groom decide to suddenly dip the bride. If you decide to move to another position, try to move smoothly while keeping your camera focused on the couple. I recommend putting your camera into a wide shot before you move; it will be easier to keep the shot steady. Try not to stand too close to the couple while you are taping. They may feel like their space has been invaded and may start acting awkwardly, which could ruin your footage. At the end of the first dance, there's almost always a kiss, so be sure to zoom in close for it. Keep the camera rolling until the end of the applause.

At the end of the dance, if the DJ announces that the food will be served shortly, then you can stop recording. If there's another activity to follow then you may want to keep the camera rolling right into the next activity. You can always edit out any unnecessary footage later.

The Blessing

Some weddings will have a blessing before the meal. For these, I recommend using a medium shot from head to waist of the person giving the blessing. The meal usually follows the blessing so, you'll be able to stop recording immediately after. Refer to the earlier section on The Meal for instructions on what to do after the blessing.

The Toasts

I've found that the toasts tend to occur almost immediately after the meal. Occasionally, there have been some toasts before the meal. Whenever possible, I will try to have the DJ tell whomever will be giving toasts to stand next to the bride and groom (see Figure 11-5). This will allow me to get footage of the person giving the toast as well as the couple's reactions. You'll find some of the reaction shots of the couple to be priceless. The three shots I use the most are close-up of the person speaking, close-up of the couple, and medium-to-wide shots that include both the speaker and the couple. Again, zoom in and out smoothly throughout the toasts.

When the toast presenters are not standing next to the couple, then focus your shots on them most of the time. If there's any way that you can zoom out wide enough to get them and the couple in the shot, you may use this shot when you feel it's appropriate, but use it sparingly.

If the toast presenter is going to be on the opposite side of the room from the couple, then stay focused on them and don't worry about getting the couple. At the end of their toast you may be able to swing around and get a shot of the couple clinking their glasses together.

The most common toast givers will be the best man and maid of honor, although there will be times when there may be more than one best man or

Figure 11-5
Toast.

maid of honor. I've taped weddings where one or both of the fathers gave a toast as well. Keep an eye on the couple during the toast whenever possible; you never know when there will be an emotional shot of them. At the end of a toast, after you've recorded the couple clinking their glasses and drinking, you may be able to get some quick shots of some of the guests clinking their glasses or applauding. These will make great reaction shots to edit with, but be sure to record each shot for at least four or five seconds; otherwise they will be too short to use. And make sure all of the toasts have been given before you stop recording.

Entertainment During the Meal

During my career, I've had several weddings that featured entertainment during the meal. The entertainment has consisted of friends or family members of the couple performing a song or a dance, performers demonstrating cultural dances, Polynesian shows, and even the wedding party performing a special choreographed dance number. If your client has plans to have mealtime entertainment, I strongly encourage you to upgrade them to a video package that includes a second videographer for the reception. It will make the footage much more interesting to watch. And without a second videographer, you won't get a chance to eat.

HELPFUL TIP: I encourage you to check in with the DJ throughout the reception to find out what the next activity will be and when it will begin so you can be sure you have enough tape and battery time left.

Since each mealtime performance is different, I can't explain how to shoot each of them in detail, but I will offer the following advice. If there's someone singing, you may want to use the guidelines for shooting toasts. If there's dancing, never zoom in on their faces. Most of the shots should be wide enough to see their feet and their heads and maybe an occasional medium shot from head to waist (see Figure 11-6). Be sure to follow the action and look for opportunities to get the bride and groom's reactions.

Dancing with the Parents

Often referred to as the father-bride or mother-groom dances, this is the portion of the reception when the father of the bride gets to dance with his daughter (see Figure 11-7) or the groom's mother gets to dance with her son.

Figure 11-6
Entertainment during the meal.

Figure 11-7
Father-bride dance.

The father-bride dance usually starts this segment. They may dance an entire song together or during the song, the groom and his mother may join in. Not every wedding has both, but be aware that it's become more common. I've even witnessed the other parents joining in at some point during the song.

Follow the guidelines I described previously for taping the first dance. Watch for a special hug at the end of the song. I recommend keeping the camera rolling after these dances as they usually lead into another ceremonial activity like the wedding party dance.

Wedding Party Dance

This is when all of the wedding party members join the bride and groom on the dance floor (see Figure 11-8). Larger wedding parties will present more of a challenge for videotaping. As I'm recording, I'll try to focus on one couple at a time using medium to close-up shots (see Figure 11-9), smoothly shifting my shot from one couple to another as I work my way in between them. If you can shoot the entire song continuously with smooth motion throughout, you may be able to use the footage in its entirety with little to no editing required. Be careful not to invade any one couple's space for very long. Tape one couple for 10 to 15 seconds and then move on to the next one. Occasionally, you may want to zoom out to wider shots featuring several couples. I will often try to end the song by zooming in on the bride and groom. Again, you may want to keep the camera rolling after the song is over in case there's another activity to follow.

Cutting the Cake

When it's time to cut the cake, try to position yourself in such a way that you can see the couple, the cake, and the area where they will be cutting (see Figure 11-10). Try to not get in the photographer's way, but make sure you get the shots you need. Most photographers will start with the bride and groom holding the knife on the cake, ready to cut, and looking at the photographer's camera. This is a good place to begin recording. You may want to start with a

Figure 11-8
Wedding party dance.

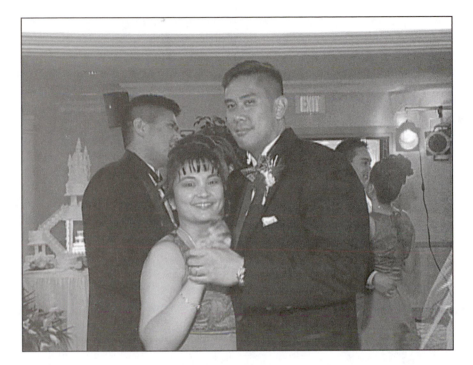

Figure 11-9
Focusing on one
couple at a time.

Figure 11-10
Framing for
cake-cutting.

close-up of the couple's faces or a wide shot of the couple with the cake; either is fine.

As they proceed to cut the cake, gradually zoom in on their hands. When they pull the piece of cake out and put it onto the plate, try to get a close-up of the cake. It will help them remember what kind of cake it was when they watch your video years from now.

Now they are ready to begin feeding the cake to each other. Zoom in to a medium, head to waist shot so you'll be able to see their hands and faces throughout the shot. Be ready to zoom out quickly should one of them feel the need to duck backwards suddenly. Continue taping until after they have kissed. You may want to continue rolling even after they have kissed just in case something spontaneous happens. You'll know it's time to stop taping when they start wiping their faces with a napkin or start to walk away from the cake table. When they are done, I will often spin around to get some reaction shots of the guests who are watching. I may focus on one or two people, then shift to someone else, and so on. Try to get at least four to five seconds of each reaction shot.

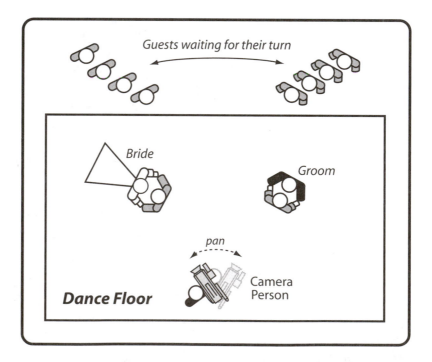

Figure 11-11
View from above showing camera position.

Honeymoon Dance (Money Dance)

The honeymoon dance, or money dance as it is often referred to, is the part of the reception when the guests will line up and take turns dancing with the bride or groom in exchange for a small donation towards the couple's honeymoon. By now, after having taped all of the various other dances, you should have a feel of how to shoot this. It can be one of the most grueling portions of the reception to videotape, but here are some tips to help make it more palatable.

Sometimes the dance will start with the couple dancing with each other until people start lining up. Start recording at the beginning of the song. After the first person has approached either the bride or groom, you should see them start to separate from each other. Position yourself between the bride and the groom in such a way that you can tape either one of them without seeing the other one (see Figure 11-11). For the rest of the honeymoon dance, take turns taping the bride dancing with someone (see Figure 11-12), then the groom (see Figure 11-13), then the bride dancing with the next person, then

Figure 11-12
Bride dancing with guest.

Figure 11-13
Groom dancing with
guest.

the groom dancing with the next person, and so your goal is to get the face of every person who dances with the bride and groom. Occasionally, you may want to shoot some of the guests waiting in line or sitting by their tables. These shots make great cutaways, but make sure you don't have the bride or groom in any of them.

After you've continuously recorded for about three to four songs, you can then pause your camera between each shot after getting about five to eight seconds of each person. In the next chapter, I'll explain how to edit these clips together. The honeymoon dance ends when there are no more people waiting to dance with either the bride or the groom or when the couple is reunited to dance with each other again.

When the dance is over, it's safe to stop taping as there will be a break in the action while they gather up the money. If you haven't already done so, this may be a good time to check your battery and the remaining time left on your tape to see if either needs to be changed before the next activity. You may also want to check in with the DJ to see when the next activity will begin.

Open Dancing

Usually there will be periods of time during the reception between activities, when the DJ or band tries to get the guests to dance. We refer to this as open dancing time. The guests get to let their hair down and have fun. Often, the first few songs of the open dancing period are the best time to get shots of the guests having a good time (see Figure 11-14). It is critical that you record some footage of this, as all couples like to see their guests having fun.

This is the time to really get creative with your shooting. Don't be afraid to experiment a little. You could try some high-angle, low-angle, and dutch-angle shots, for example. Have fun with it.

Shots to Look For

There are some key opportunities during the open dancing to get some great shots if you know what to look for. Be on the lookout for group participation songs (YMCA, electric slide, conga lines, etc.). Also, watch for when the guests form two lines and one or two people at a time strut their stuff as they cruise

Figure 11-14
Open dancing.

from one end to the other between the two lines. Don't forget to get grandparents, aunts, uncles, and parents "shaking their booty," as these are priceless moments. And, be on the lookout for things like the bride dancing with her grandfather or brother.

How do you know when you have enough footage of open dancing? When you notice that song after song seems to have the same 12 people on the dance floor. Or when you have over 30 minutes of dancing and much of it is not that interesting. After you've shot and edited several weddings, you'll start to get a feel for how much dance footage you'll need.

Bouquet Toss

Before I continue with the bouquet toss, I want to remind you that by this time in the reception, you may need to check the batteries in your wireless transmitters and receivers. Are you still receiving your feed from the DJ or band? All right, now on to the bouquet.

If you haven't already checked in with the DJ to find out when they will be throwing the bouquet, you can listen for clues. For example, when the DJ announces for all of the single ladies to come to the dance floor, that's a good sign that the bouquet toss will be happening soon. The DJ will usually put the single ladies on one side of the dance floor and the bride on the other with her back to the ladies.

I recommend positioning yourself in front of the bride and off to the side so you can see the bride's face, bouquet, throwing arm, and the ladies behind her. Be sure to have your camera shot wide enough to see the bouquet as she releases it over her head (see Figure 11-15). Also, keep in mind that the bouquet will usually arc up towards the ceiling, so be sure you can get that too.

It's not uncommon for the DJ to count to three and for the bride to fake throwing the bouquet. Then they'll start over again. Most brides will actually throw it on the second try. Stay with the bouquet as it travels through the air and hopefully lands in someone's hands. As soon as the bouquet arrives at its final destination, zoom in quickly on the person who caught it using a head-to-waist shot and stay on them until they walk off the dance floor. Some photographers may have this person pose with the bride for a picture; it's up to you if you want to record this. You may stop recording now.

Garter Toss

If they have one, the garter toss will usually follows the bouquet toss. You'll hear a similar announcement as the DJ asks for all of the single men to come to the dance floor. Someone will bring a chair to the middle of the dance floor for the bride to sit on. There have been a few instances when the DJ had the bride sit on someone's back or knees, but usually it's a chair.

The groom is then instructed to remove the garter from his bride. I recommend taping this from a side view. This will allow you to get both the groom's face as well as the bride's face during this part. Continue rolling at least until the groom has successfully retrieved the garter. You may either stop recording here to reposition yourself for the actual toss or keep rolling until the whole process is complete.

Figure 11-15
Bouquet toss.

After the garter has been retrieved, the groom will stand across the dance floor from the single men with his back turned as well, just like the bride did. From this point on, I suggest shooting the same way you did for the bouquet toss (see Figure 11-16). You may want to move to the other side of the groom if you like, but stay in front of him so you can see everything as before. Be aware that the garter doesn't fly as well as the bouquet. Follow the throw and again zoom in on the person who catches it and keep rolling until they leave the dance floor.

Special Dances or Activities

Some weddings may include unique or special activities such as a special tribute dance. Use the guidelines I've provided so far; they should cover most situations.

Interviews

I ask all of my clients if they want me to interview or record messages from their guests. Many videographers and clients have referred to these messages as interviews even though there may not be any actual questions being asked. Should your client want them, here are some ideas on how to get them. After many of the main activities are finished and you've recorded some open dancing, this could be a good time to do the interviews. You need to make sure you'll have enough time before the next activity, so check in with the DJ to find out when the next event will happen. If there's at least 15 minutes before the next activity, then proceed with some interviews.

Get out your handheld microphone. If you are using a wired microphone, then plug it into your camera. If you're using a wireless mic, then make sure the receiver is connected to your camera and turned on. Make sure it's not on the same frequency as the transmitter you connected to the DJ. Turn on the transmitter on the handheld mic. Now test the mic to make sure it's working properly. If everything is functioning correctly, then you're ready to start taping messages.

Figure 11-16
Garter toss.

One popular method I've used for messages is to first scout out a good (preferably scenic) location outside of the main room that the reception is being held in. Weather permitting, outdoors is preferred, but the main things I'm looking for are to be away from the loud music, a little bit of privacy, a nice-looking background, and easy access from the party. Once I have found the location, I will have the DJ announce to the guests that we will be doing interviews and personal messages at this time. He or she will then instruct them on where to go. I will set up at the location and wait for people to come out. If no one comes or only a few come out, then I'll have the DJ make another announcement. There have been some weddings when this doesn't work.

Another popular method I've used is to have the couple recommend someone, or I'll get the best man or maid of honor to go and get people and send them out to my location.

When the guest comes out and is ready to record their message, I'll hand them the mic and instruct them to wait for my signal before they start talking. Then I'll make sure I have them in focus and start recording (see Figure 11-17).

I like to record a few seconds before I give them the cue to begin talking. I will also record a few more seconds after they have finished. These extra few seconds will come in handy when it's time to edit. I always thank them as I retrieve my mic from them.

Sometimes you may have a guest who's a little nervous. I'll ask them simple questions to get them comfortable, like, "How are you enjoying the wedding?" or "How do you know the couple?" You'd be amazed at how much people will open up to you once you've shown them what a nice person you are.

I've found that sometimes it can be real handy to have the interview mic with you earlier in the event. I've had a few guests ask to record their message during the cocktail hour.

Other Key Shots to Look For

As you get to know who the important guests are, such as grandparents, aunts, uncles, or family from out of town, be on the lookout for special moments involving any of them. Ring bearers and flower girls may also provide

Figure 11-17
Guest Interview.

some great shots, for example, the ring bearer dancing with the flower girl. Kids' antics sometimes add humor to the video.

The End of the Day

If your client contracted you for the entire day, then you'll probably be taping until the end of the reception or at least until the couple leaves. Some couples stay in the hotel that the reception is being held at, so there won't be much of a good-bye to shoot. Other couples may have planned a more elaborate farewell, such as having the guests hold sparklers as the couple exits the building or getting into a limo. My advice is to be ready for anything and make sure you shoot from in front of the couple. You'll be able to see their faces and whatever the guests may be doing while the couple exits. Use your best judgment for shooting the couple getting into the limo.

If the client doesn't have anything special planned, then you'll want to be sure to tell them good-bye before you leave and ask them if there's anything else they want you to tape before you go. I will also wish them "Congratulations" and tell them what a great wedding it was. Then it's time to pack everything up. You may want to take out the checklist of your equipment so you won't accidentally leave anything behind. When you take the tape out of the camera, be sure to activate the record inhibit tab so you can't accidentally record over it.

Chapter 12
Editing the Video

Before you begin the editing phase of the video, do you have everything you need to complete the job? For example, will you be using any photographs supplied by the client for a photo montage? Do you have all of the music you're going to use? Since most of the editing will be done on a computer, you don't want to load all of the footage onto your hard drives until you've received everything you need to complete the project. If another project comes along that is ready for editing, you'd have to delete this entire project from the hard drive and then recapture it again later.

Typical Video Layout

Every videographer has their own unique style, but many of the wedding videos I've watched seem to have a similar structure. They'll start with an opening montage followed by the ceremony followed by the post-ceremony montage. Then comes the reception followed by a closing recap montage that may or may not contain credits. I'll use this format to keep the explanation of the process simple.

Pre-Ceremony (Opening) Montage

In Chapter 9, I talked about what to videotape before the ceremony. These are the items we will use to create the pre-ceremony montage. In many of my videos, I would start with a shot of the front of the church and use a titling program to put the bride and groom's names over the footage along with their wedding date.

I might then go to a shot of the sign with the church's name on it. These serve as establishing shots that let the viewer know where this event is about to take place.

Then I'd proceed using the various clips of the guests arriving, bride and groom getting ready, shots of the church, and photo session. I usually try to keep the length of this montage down to about the length of one song (three to five minutes). Sometimes I'll superimpose the invitation over some video for a nice look. At the end of this montage, I'll dissolve to the beginning of the ceremony. All of these clips will be edited together using transitions, primarily dissolves, and bound together with music. Now this brings up a very controversial question regarding the use of music. Before I can continue I must insert this disclaimer. **[Disclaimer: I am not an attorney and I cannot offer legal advice. You should consult an attorney regarding the legal use of music.]**

Types of Music

There are some companies selling royalty-free or buyout music. When you purchase this type of music you are also buying the rights to use it however you want to use it. These are commonly used in videos that will be mass-produced and distributed. There are other companies selling music on a contract basis. For example, you pay them a fee every time you use one of their songs (sometimes referred to as a "needle-drop" fee), or they'll sell you the rights to use any song in their library for a limited period of time, such as for one year. These are also commonly used in mass-distributed videos or videos for commercial use. Both of these categories of music may be used in wedding videos as long as you have legally purchased the rights to use them.

The popular music played on the radio and sold in stores is classified as copyrighted music. Copyright laws state that you may not reproduce or distribute copyrighted music without written permission from the legal owner of the copyrights. Technically, using these songs in your wedding videos is a violation of copyright laws. However, there are many who believe that under the "fair use" provision, it is acceptable for someone to make a copy of a song that they purchased legally, for their own use and not for commercial distribution or profit. This could imply that it might be okay if a client wanted to use a song from their own collection of music (obtained legitimately) for their own video.

The final decision as to which category of music to use for your videos rests entirely on you.

The Ceremony

As I mentioned earlier, I will typically dissolve from the opening montage into the beginning of the ceremony when the grandparents or parents begin their walk down the aisle. The method for editing the ceremony will vary depending on how many cameras were used to record it. Including most or all of the ceremony in your final edit is referred to as the long-form edit. The following descriptions refer to the long-form edit. I'll cover the short-form edit a little later.

Capturing the Video From Your Tape Into the Computer

You may need to consult the manual for your editing software for instructions on how to capture video. If your software permits, capture the video as one continuous clip.

I recommend using an audio mixer while you're capturing the video. Your audio mixer should be connected in the following manner. Using the audio cables from your playback VCR, connect the left output cable to one input source on the audio mixer. Connect the right output cable to a separate input source that has its own separate volume control. You should connect two output cables from the mixer into your computer left and right input jacks. This configuration will allow you to mix both of your audio tracks together and send the resulting mix out to both channels of your video. Depending on how you used your camera's audio inputs, you will now be able to mix them as needed while you capture the footage into your computer. For example, in situations when you recorded the groom's mic on one channel and used the camera's mic for ambient sound on the other channel, you may want to emphasize the groom's mic more and turn the ambient sound down. While capturing the ceremony footage, I tend to keep the ambient sound low, using the other channel as my primary audio.

If you don't have an audio mixer then you'll have to use your editing software to adjust each audio channel after you've captured the video.

One-Camera Ceremonies

If you only used one camera for videotaping the ceremony and you kept it rolling throughout the entire ceremony, then you may not have a lot of editing to do. Assuming that you videotaped the entire ceremony using only smooth camera movements, your editing should only require a dissolve from the opening montage at the beginning and fade to black, white, or the post-ceremony montage at the end. And then you're done with the ceremony. The only additional editing you may choose to incorporate in your ceremony involves a technique referred to as time compression. This is a popular technique for shortening the processional. I'll explain this process a little later.

Two-Camera Ceremonies

Most videographers prefer to have two cameras for taping ceremonies. In order to edit a two-camera ceremony, you'll need to capture the footage from both cameras into your editing computer. I will usually name the clips "Ceremony-Camera1" and "Ceremony-Camera2." This way, I'll always know which camera angle was used for each clip. You could also use "front camera" or "back camera," if it's easier for you. After importing both clips into your editing software, you'll need to synchronize (sync) the clips with each other on the timeline.

First, you'll need to drag one of the clips into your timeline. Then drag the second clip onto the superimpose line (or secondary track) of the timeline and have both clips start at the same point of your timeline. Most editing programs will allow you to lower the transparency of one track so that it is superimposed over the other track, allowing you to see both. Another option is to use a picture-in-picture or a split-screen transition so that you can see the video from both clips simultaneously.

Methods for Synchronizing Clips

One popular method is to look for a part of the video where both cameras are focused on the same subject or the same section of the church and look for a flash from the photographer's camera. Be aware that there may be several flashes, so you'll have to try to find the same flash for synchronizing the clips together.

Another method involves looking for the same activity occurring in both clips where both cameras have the same person in their shots. Then compare the movements of that person in both clips. You should be able to line up their action in both clips to the point where they match exactly.

Or you can try comparing the audio tracks for both clips and attempt to match them up that way. After you've synchronized the clips, you're ready to start editing.

Choosing Clips to Use

There are different ways to edit the ceremony; here's how I've done it. I'll use the picture-in-picture or split-screen transition in my editing software so I can see both clips at the same time. Then I'll look through each clip and cut out any and all sections that are not usable. For example, if one of the cameras was out of focus or was jerked around abruptly, I know that footage won't be usable at all so, I'll delete it. Finally, I'll go back through the timeline and decide which of the two camera angles has the best shot at any given point in the ceremony. Here are some tips to help you determine the best camera angle for each key segment of the ceremony.

- Processional—the front camera will provide most of the footage for this portion of the ceremony.
- Opening comments from the minister, scripture readings, and the sermon—the back camera should be the primary camera with occasional cutaways from the front camera.
- Vows and ring exchange—you'll be going back and forth a lot between both cameras. Whichever camera has the best shot, use it.
- Unity candle lighting—the camera with the best view. You may be able to alternate between the cameras but not very much.
- Singers and musicians—whichever camera has the best shot.
- The kiss—whichever camera has the best shot.
- Pronouncement and recessional—the back camera will provide most of the footage for both of these with an occasional cutaway to the front camera, if necessary.

If I find a section of the ceremony where I had to delete footage from both cameras because both cameras had bad shots, then I'll look through the rest of the footage for a cutaway clip that I can insert instead. Front camera close-up shots of the bride and groom watching the minister work great for this. Once I've narrowed down the video to just the best camera angles for every part of the ceremony, then I'll go back and drop in basic cross-dissolves to fade back and forth from one camera to the other. For the recessional, I'll use most of the footage from the back camera. After the family and wedding party have exited past the camera, I'll dissolve to black, white, or the post-ceremony montage. Just as with the one-camera edit, you'll have to decide if you want to use any time-compression strategies.

Multiple-Camera Ceremonies

When you use three or more cameras to record the ceremony, the editing process is essentially the same as the two-camera edit. You'll need to sync up all of the camera clips first and remove the bad clips. You may want to edit the main two cameras together first and then go back and add the others.

Time Compression

The editing technique of compressing time is great for shortening a wedding video or making it more interesting. To illustrate how it works, I'll use the ceremony processional as an example. Let's say you're taping a wedding that has eight bridesmaids and eight groomsmen. You're taping in a church with a really long aisle, and the wedding party is walking down the aisle two at a time, one bridesmaid escorted by one groomsman. This portion of the video could last five to ten minutes. We'll assume that as you were recording with your front camera, you zoomed in on the first couple at the back of the church and gradually zoomed out as they came down the aisle, getting closer to you. After they walked out of your shot, you proceeded to zoom in on the next couple and followed them down the aisle and continued this process for the rest of the couples.

For editing purposes, we'll keep the clip of the first couple walking down the aisle. For each of the rest of the couples, let's remove the portion of the video while the camera was zooming in on the next couple. In order to compress time, when each couple reaches the front of the church we will dissolve into our shot of the next couple, after the zoom. At this point, we have removed several seconds of video. Now, if in fact the church had a really long aisle, then you might want to remove the footage of each couple up to the point, let's say, when they've reached the middle of the church. This will remove even more time from the video.

As long as we make sure to use dissolve transitions between each clip, the viewer will not care that we removed portions of the video. They'll get the idea of what we're trying to show them. Time compression is a very powerful technique for editing wedding videos.

Short-Form Edits

Using an advanced version of the time-compression technique I just described, you can create a short-form edit of the ceremony, also known as a highlights version. The goal of a short-form edit is to give the viewer a sense of what happened at the ceremony without having to show them all of it. Usually, you want to try to get this down to around 15 minutes or so in length.

By now you may be wondering, "How do we reduce a one-hour ceremony to 15 minutes or so?" That's a good question. Here's the secret. First, you have to have a good understanding as to what the really important parts of the ceremony are. In my experience, I've discovered that the processional (especially the bride's entrance), the vows and ring exchange, lighting of the unity candle, the kiss, pronouncement, and recessional are the most important segments. However, if the couple had friends or family reading scriptures or performing songs, then a portion of those should be added. Use your best judgment as to what you think will be important to the couple. As you gain more experience with weddings, you'll get a feel for what's important.

The simplest way to create the short-form edit would be to remove all of the clips that don't fall into the above categories and put dissolves between the remaining clips. You may want to fade in and fade out the audio between each of the segments you decide to keep. As you gain more experience with your editing, you'll become more creative in how you edit the different sections together. I've been able to edit my short-form videos to the point where you can't really tell that anything is missing.

If you also edit the reception footage using the short-form edit, then you'll create a highlights version of the entire wedding day with a video that will only take 30 to 40 minutes to watch. Clients in today's busy world really appreciate this. Most of their friends don't want to sit and watch a two-hour video of someone else's wedding. Over the years, the highlights version of the wedding video has been the most popular option my company has ever offered.

Post-Ceremony Montage

The post-ceremony montage is similar to the pre-ceremony montage except you will be using the footage you shot after the ceremony but before the reception. Some videographers have combined this montage with their preliminary shots from the reception, before the grand entrance, to make one montage instead of two.

The Reception

If you chose not to combine footage, then you may want to create a separate montage using the preliminary footage you've shot of the reception location, decorations, or cocktail hour. For this montage, follow the same instructions on how to edit the pre-ceremony montage, using these reception clips.

Capturing and Naming Video Clips

Depending on the capabilities of your editing system, you may want to edit the reception as a separate project from the ceremony. While videotaping the reception, your camera should have recorded two channels of audio, one for the ambient sound and one from the DJ. Using an audio mixer, you'll be able to mix the audio between the two channels to create just the right balance. For example, when the DJ introduces the wedding party, you can turn up the DJ feed to hear the announcements better. Then you can turn up the ambient channel to hear the guests cheering and applauding. The mixer will allow you to change the sound mix as you need to in order to follow the activity of the reception. Here are a few pointers on which channel to favor for the different reception activities (DJ or ambient):

· Grand entrance—DJ for the introductions, ambient during the applause
· Blessing—DJ

- All dances—DJ with just enough of the ambient so you can faintly hear the people in the background
- Toasts— You should emphasize the DJ a little more, but keep the ambient loud enough to hear the guests laughing or reacting to the toast.
- Cake-cutting—ambient with the DJ in the background
- Bouquet and garter toss—Both about equal, ambient to hear the guests and the DJ to hear what is said to the crowd
- Interviews—Interview mic only, but with some ambient. If you have a large group involved in the same interview then, you may want to bring up the ambient more.

When you start capturing your reception footage, capture each activity as a separate clip. Whenever you stopped recording with your camera will be the end of a clip. When you started recording again, that will be the beginning of the next clip.

Name each clip with a sequential number and an appropriate name. For example, I might label my clips as follows: grand entrance clip as "01-GrandEntrance," first dance as "02-FirstDance," Toast as "03-Toasts," father-bride dance as "04-FatherBride," and so on. The names will help identify the contents of each clip. The numbering system will force the editing software to keep them in the order they occurred at the reception.

The interviews I will capture separately, using the following method for naming them: Interview01, Interview02, Interview03, etc. I want each interview to be a separate clip from the others. I'll explain why in a moment.

Putting the Clips Together

After all of the clips have been captured into your computer, drag each clip onto the timeline in numerical order. In Chapter 11, I made several references to shooting the various activities in their entirety. For every activity that you were able to capture as one continuous smooth, flowing shot, you should be able to use the entire shot in the final video. Trim the beginning of each clip to the most appropriate point for it to start. For example, if you started taping before the DJ announced the next activity and you had some additional footage with nothing happening, you may want to remove this portion and start when something starts to happen. Trim the end of each clip in a similar manner to remove all of the uneventful footage.

In order to make the transition smoother from one clip to the next, you may want to select a transition to put between each clip. Earlier, I mentioned that I prefer to make each interview a separate clip. This will allow me to insert one interview between each reception activity or clip to break up the reception coverage. This makes for a great transition between activities. For example, after the first dance, I will cut to an interview. After the interview, I'll go to the father-bride dance. Then I'll go to another interview, and so on. As you continue assembling the clips, I recommend cross-fading the audio at every junction between each clip. This will eliminate abrupt changes in the audio that make the video seem choppy.

Editing the Honeymoon Dance

In the previous chapter, I suggested shooting a series of clips alternating between the bride and the groom during the honeymoon dance. Capture the entire honeymoon dance segment as one continuous clip even though you may have stopped recording several times during the dance. Drag this clip onto your timeline and lock the audio track (refer to your editing software manual on how to do this). Now you're going to cut the video track into several smaller clips (between five and eight seconds each) that will show the faces of each of the guests that danced with the bride and groom. Alternating equally between bride and groom, connect all of the video clips together using dissolves. When you have finished this process, the video portion of the honeymoon dance should be significantly shorter than the original clip. You should notice that the audio clip is now longer than the video. Cut or trim the audio to match the video and be sure to fade in at the beginning and fade out at the end.

Editing the Garter Toss

At most weddings, there will be a pause in the action between the groom's retrieval of the garter and when he finally throws it. Whether you recorded this down time or not, you may want to edit so that you go from the end of the retrieval directly to the beginning of the toss. I recommend using a transition between these two clips to smooth out the flow of the video.

The End of the Reception

Finding the right scene to end the reception coverage can be challenging. I have used a slow dance that I've shot during the open dancing or a sentimental interview to wrap up the reception coverage, even though it may not have been the last thing I videotaped. At the end of the clip, I usually fade to black before proceeding to the closing montage.

Short-Form Editing

Creating a short-form edit for the reception can be a little more challenging than for the ceremony. While you may find that some of your clips can be deleted for the short-form edit, there may be several that you won't be able to cut due to their importance. Some examples of important clips from the reception include the first dance, father-bride dance, mother-groom dance, toasts, cake cutting, and bouquet and garter toss.

An alternate solution is to find a way to reduce the length of each of these clips. Try using some time-compression techniques to reduce each of the segments to about one minute or so in length. There will be some clips that you won't be able to cut down that much; don't worry about it. The goal is to get the reception down to about 15 to 20 minutes. Again, as you gain more experience, you'll get better at this.

Closing Recap Montage

The closing or recap montage usually runs about three to five minutes long and is sort of like a mini-highlights video. It will often contain key clips from the wedding day, featuring some of most emotional moments like the exchange of vows or the toasts, moments that contain the most emotion. These clips along with some of your artistic shots of the bride and groom can be creatively blended together to produce a dramatic closing to the video. Using effects like slow-motion, soft focus, letterboxing, or even converting some footage to black and white can add a cinematic look to the montage. The purpose of this montage is to recap the day's events quickly but leave the viewer feeling very emotionally touched. You want to make the viewer say, "Wow, that was an awesome video." Incorporating credits listing the wedding party during this montage adds a nice touch. Be as creative as you can while editing this montage.

Essential Editing Tips

What to Edit Out and What to Leave In

As editors, we are constantly faced with the dilemma of deciding what footage will end up "on the cutting room floor." Here is how I approach the decision-making process.

I will ask myself:

· If this was my wedding video, would I want this footage left in?
· Does this clip contain any footage of an important relative or friend? Do I have any other footage of this person? Is this footage better or worse than the other footage that I have of this person?
· Do I already have too much footage of the people in this clip? Is this footage better or worse than the other footage that I have of these people?
· Does this clip contain anything that adds to the video?
· Is the material in this clip suitable for all audiences? If not, will the couple still want it included, maybe in a separate section at the end?
· Is there anything in this clip that may reflect badly on the wedding?

These are some of the questions I ponder as I'm editing. I think you get the general idea of how to make decisions for your editing. I suggest that you don't delete a clip just for the sake of deleting it; have a good reason.

If you come across a clip that you really can't decide whether it's appropriate to leave in or not, you may want to contact your client and ask their opinion. Be aware, though, that this might open the door for them wanting to be included in the entire editing process. This is not generally a good idea as it could double the amount of time you'll spend editing the video. Since most wedding videographers do not get paid by the hour, it could cost you more than you know.

Including Photos

Many videographers have included photos of the bride and groom from their past in various sections of the video. I've used them to create a sort of vignette (pronounced *vin-yét*) where I insert pictures of the bride with her father during the father-bride dance. These are pictures featuring just the two of them at different stages of the bride's life. It can provide a fun way to spice up the video.

Pacing

One of the most important aspects of storytelling is referred to as pacing. Pacing greatly affects how the story is told. If your pacing is too slow, you might bore the viewer. If the pacing is too fast, they won't be able to keep up. Many of the people who watch videos today are used to the fast pace used in many of the current movies and television programs, where the shot changes about every two to three seconds. With the limited amount of cameras we use for taping weddings (and the limited budget), it's much harder to be able to maintain that sort of pace; we don't have enough different camera angles. I don't recommend changing shots that often for wedding videos.

Movies from 30 and 40 years ago had single shots that lasted most of the scene. Today's audiences might get bored with that, so I've tried to create a compromise between the two styles. I will let the content dictate the pace. In other words, I will use what is happening in the video at the time to determine the pace of that portion of the video. For example, during the ceremony, much of the action on the screen is rather slow, so I will use dissolves and keep the shots on the screen longer, 10 to 30 seconds. For the reception, some of the scenes may feature people dancing to a fast-paced song, so I may just want to cut from one shot to another within five seconds.

Varying the pace throughout the video is more likely to keep your viewer's interest without wearing them out. Viewers don't need to see two minutes of the bride putting on her veil. Ten seconds is enough time for the viewer to get the idea of what is happening before moving on to the next clip or scene. On the other hand, it may take the groom two minutes to say his vows, and you should keep all of it. For the montages, the shots can be kept fairly brief, but for the ceremony and reception, it's okay to use longer shots as long as the content is interesting.

Jump Cuts

Jump cuts are when the flow of the video is disrupted by a break in continuity in time. Let's say you have a continuous video clip of a news anchor delivering the news, and you remove one or two seconds from the middle of the clip. Now you push the two new clips together and play them. You might notice that at the place of the missing video, the anchor's head "jumps" to a different position. Or you have a scene where someone is standing by a window holding a glass and the next shot, from a different angle, shows the same person with no glass in their hand. It's as if the glass just disappeared. These are examples of jump cuts.

For obvious reasons, you need to avoid jump cuts in your wedding videos. One way to avoid this is to use a transition. A commonly used transition is a dissolve (sometimes referred to as a cross-dissolve), where one video clip disappears as another clip appears. The first clip dissolves into the second clip. Most editing programs have a variety of different transitions to choose from.

Use of Transitions

In editing wedding videos, I've tried to stick with the basic cuts and dissolves for most of my transitions between clips. They never go out of style, and movies and television programs seem to do the same as well. I may throw in a few really cool transitions during the reception to keep the pace lively. The art of storytelling is not contained in the transitions or special effects; the story is told through the content of the video. Producing a wedding video is all about telling the story of one special day in a couple's lives. The better you tell the story, the more you get paid and the more referrals you'll receive.

Use of Special Effects

What are special effects? In wedding videos, slow-motion, soft-focus filters, flashes of white, and converting video to black and white are examples of special effects. Most of the video filters offered in many of today's editing programs are considered effects.

You can always tell when a videographer has just purchased a new editing system or editing-related software by the quantity of special effects he or she uses in their next video. It seems that every time we get a new toy, we can't wait to play with it. A true professional will know when a special effect should be used and when it shouldn't. Never use a special effect without a good reason for it. And *never* overuse them! For example, I've watched too many wedding demos that contained nothing but shot after shot in slow motion. I admit that adding slow motion can really add drama or emotion to a scene but, a four-minute video that contains nothing but slow-motion shots will feel like a 10-minute video to the viewer.

EDITOR'S RULE #1: Never overuse any one transition or special effect. Just like too much salt can ruin a good steak, too many repeated effects can ruin a good video.

Use effects like you would use seasoning on food. A little seasoning brings out the flavor; too much seasoning and you can no longer tell what you're eating. My simple rule of thumb regarding transitions or effects is to *never* overuse any one effect. Occasional slow-motion is fine, but not constant. Occasional soft focus is fine but not every other shot.

Cross-Fading Audio

Cross-fading audio is where you fade out the audio (lower the volume) from your first source as you're fading in the audio (increasing the volume) from the next source. DJs have been doing this for years. For example, when you hear one song getting quieter while another song is getting louder at the same time, this is referred to as cross-fading.

When you are putting two video clips that contain audio together that came from two different sources or two different periods of time, they will sound very rough as the audio changes from one clip to another. Use a cross-fade to smooth out the transition from one clip to the other.

Creating the Edit Master

After you've completed the editing of the video, it's time to create the edit master. I encourage the use of a digital videotape format for storing the edited master of your video in addition to a DVD master. Current digital tape formats include Digi-Beta (Digital Betacam), DVCAM, DVCPRO, DV, and miniDV. I currently use DVCAM since I also shoot with that format. You may be wondering why I suggest both formats. The first reason is that DVDs have not been proven to last. There have already been reports of DVDs that have begun coming apart. The second reason is that production of a DVD requires the video to be compressed and therefore lose some of its picture quality. It's possible that soon there may be a new format for archiving video that is better than DVD. Maintaining a digital videotape master will allow you to put your customer's video onto whatever new format comes along without losing any picture quality. And, finally, should something happen to either your DVD or the customer's DVD that prohibits the DVD from playing correctly, you'll be able to create another copy of the video without having to re-edit it from scratch (assuming you still had the raw footage).

What About the Raw Footage?

Over the years, many videographers have been asked by their clients if they can have the raw (unedited) footage. I have always felt that I would not be comfortable giving the client all of my footage for three main reasons. First, I don't want them to see any mistakes I may have made. Second, if they ever showed the raw footage to their friends, their friends might think, "This videographer did a horrible job." And, third, I am effectively giving away my rights to the video. When a photographer takes a photo, he or she owns the copyrights to that photo and they can do whatever they want with it. They could sell copies of it, use it for demos, enter it into a contest, or whatever they choose. Like photographers, videographers own the rights to the videos they shoot and produce.

Some videographers are more open to the idea of editing a highlights version (short form) of the video and then giving the client the raw footage. They feel the client should have all of the footage from their wedding. For anyone choosing to give their client the raw footage, I would strongly encourage that you remove any bad or unprofessional footage that you don't want anyone to see before turning it over to the client. Make them a new, slightly edited tape of their footage. The final decision will be up to you as to what you want to do with your footage.

Chapter 13
Packaging and Delivering the Video

Now that you've finished editing the video, it's time to create the customer's copies. Currently, the two main choices of formats your customers can use are DVD and VHS. As of this writing, most of my customers have been asking for DVDs. I'll begin with the VHS copies first.

VHS Copies of the Video

VHS is the easiest format to make copies on but offers the lowest quality of video. In the previous chapter, I mentioned the idea of creating a digital videotape master. Whichever type of recorder you used to create the master can be connected to a standard stereo VHS VCR. As you play the master tape, you'll record onto a blank VHS tape. This process is what we refer to as a linear dub. You may not need to make VHS copies very often, but don't be surprised if someone asks for one. When you've finished recording the copy onto the VHS tape, don't forget to pop out the tab on the shell of the tape. This will prevent the customer from accidentally recording over it. All copies should be labeled and packaged to look as professional as possible.

Labels for VHS Tapes

Every VHS tape you provide to a customer should have a label on it stating what is on the tape in the form of a title. For example, you might have "The Wedding of Mary and John" followed by the wedding date. Don't forget to include your company name, logo, phone number and web site address. Do *not* write the titles on the labels by hand; use a computer printer to print the labels. And, do *not* use the labels that often come with the tapes you buy from the store that have the brand name of the tape on them. Either of these actions will make you look like an amateur. You can purchase blank inkjet or laser-printable VHS tape labels from Veriad or by calling 1-800-423-4643.

Cases for VHS Tapes

There are two types of cases available for VHS tapes, cardboard sleevesand vinyl cases.

Cardboard Sleeves

There are simple sleeves that consist of one solid color. Sample colors include white, black, red, green, yellow, and purple. Then there are sleeves that contain nice graphic artwork. Commercially produced movies, sold in stores, have custom-designed artwork on their sleeves. You could have a custom sleeve designed for your project, but they can get expensive as you'll need to have someone design the artwork, and then usually you'll need to order a minimum of 1,000 sleeves from a printing company. Instead, there are predesigned sleeves that have some nice artwork and a title that says something like "Our Wedding Day." You can purchase the predesigned sleeves or the single-color sleeves from ProVideo Training through their web site at www.provideotraining.com or call 1-877-362-0741.

Vinyl Cases

Vinyl cases usually have a clear sleeve around the outside so that custom-designed artwork can be slid into them, creating a professional looking case. You can have your sleeve inserts custom-designed or you can design your own and print it using a color inkjet printer. The vinyl cases may be purchased from Polyline Corporation at-1-800-701-5865.

DVD Copies of the Video

There are two basic methods for creating DVDs, "authored" and "unauthored" (or nonauthored). Currently, there are several types of DVD media on the market for recording purposes, including DVD-RAM, DVD+RW, DVD-RW, DVD+R, and DVD-R. Whether you create your DVDs using the authored or unauthored method, the most compatible disc format you should be using is called DVD-R (DVD minus R). None of these formats are guaranteed to play in every DVD player, but the DVD-R format will play in more players than the others.

For instructions on how to produce authored or unauthored DVDs, refer to Chapter 4.

Labeling the DVD

Using a laser or inkjet printer, you can customize the DVD label by including the title of the video along with your company name, logo, phone number, and web site address. There are two ways to label a DVD: printing directly onto the disc or printing onto a label that attaches to the disc. I don't recommend using the labels that you peel off and stick on the DVDs since the labels can come off the disc. When you have a disc in someone's DVD player spinning around at several hundred revolutions per minute, the last thing you want to have happen is for a label to peel off and get wrapped up inside the player, causing damage.

I recommend using DVDs that an inkjet printer can print directly onto. That way there's no label to peel off inside the DVD player. The inkjet-printable discs have become more widely available at places that sell blank DVDs. Just make sure it is a DVD-R disc.

When you're designing your labels, try not to create a design that results in a lot of ink being printed on one particular area of the disc. The design should allow for fairly even distribution of ink. Too much ink in one particular spot may cause the disc to be unbalanced while it spins inside the player, and that could result in problems during the playback of the disc.

Cases for DVDs

There are many different types of packaging for DVDs, including paper sleeves, clamshell cases, jewel cases, cardboard sleeves, and the commonly recognized vinyl DVD movie case that we're used to seeing with most DVD movies sold in stores. This is the one I recommend the most since, customers are already used to the idea that these cases contain DVD movies or videos there's little chance they'll mistake it for a CD.

As with the VHS vinyl case, the vinyl DVD movie case also has a sleeve that wraps around the outside. There are some nice-looking, generic-type sleeve inserts you can purchase that have phrases like "Our Wedding" already included in the design. These sleeves are available at www.provideotraining.com, or you can print your own custom sleeve inserts with your inkjet printer.

Designing Your Own Cover

If you want to design your own sleeve inserts, make sure they look professional. Cases that look unprofessional may cause your client to feel like they received an inferior product even if the video looks good. Often people may prejudge the quality of the video based on how the packaging looks.

When designing the cover, make sure to include a title, for example, "The Wedding of Julie and Pete—April 21, 2005." You may want to repeat the title or a portion of it across the spine of the case. I always put my company logo along with the company name, phone number and web site address on the lower portion of the back of the case. You may also want to include some frames from the video in the cover design. I've taken one of the frames and used Photoshop to blur the image and make it the background for the entire cover. Be creative, but make sure it looks professional. And a word of caution: if you print your own sleeve inserts, make sure to let them dry before inserting them into the sleeve.

Do You Need to Shrink-Wrap?

Whenever you buy a music CD or a DVD movie at the store, there is always some clear plastic wrapped around the case that you have to remove to open the package. Sometimes the packages are wrapped in a plastic known as shrink-wrap. There are machines you can buy that will allow you to shrink-wrap your own DVDs or VHS tapes one at a time, making them look more like the ones you buy at the store. Do you need to shrink-wrap your videos? It's not necessary, and I know many videographers who don't. You may if you like, but don't feel obligated.

Delivering the Video

If your client came to your place of business for the original consultation, then there's nothing wrong with them coming back to pick up the video. If you went to their home for the consultation, then you may want to deliver the videos to their place. You should have some sort of receipt or document for them to sign verifying that they have received the videos from you. This is to protect you from any claims that may come up later from customers claiming that they never received their videos. I will usually print out the actual invoice for the job and have them sign the bottom.

I inform each and every client that they have one week to make any requests for changes to be made to their video. Ideally, this is to address the possibility that I may have accidentally spelled someone's name wrong in the video. I'll let them know that all of my videos are edited by computer and that they use up a lot of hard drive space. Since I'll need the space for my next project, I can't leave their video project on the drives too long. I also inform them that I am willing to make changes that are relatively easy at no additional charge. If they want substantial changes or major re-edits, then there may be additional editing charges applied. If they want to request changes after the week and after I've deleted the project from my hard drives, then there definitely will be editing charges added and it may cost even more since I'll have to recapture all of the footage back into the computer.

Customer Survey

When you deliver the video to your client, you should give them a self-addressed, stamped envelope along with a customer survey form to fill out and send back to you after they have watched their video. This form should ask them questions as to how they liked their video, your service, along with any suggestions they may have on how you could improve your service. You may want to offer them some sort of incentive for sending this back to you, such as an extra copy of the video for free. You'll need this feedback to ensure that your clients are truly happy with your service. If you assume that you are doing a good job and in reality you have unhappy customers, it could eventually put you out of business. This happens more often then you think. When a business has no idea of how its customers feel about the service they've received, the company is really in trouble.

Don't assume that a dissatisfied customer will automatically tell you there's a problem. Think back to the last time you received bad service from a business. Did you bother to tell them? Unhappy customers are 10 times more likely to tell their friends about a bad experience with a company than a good experience, regardless of whether they actually informed the business or not.

Follow-up is so important that I would even suggest contacting your customers a few weeks after they've received their video to make sure everything is fine.

Chapter 14
Add-On Sales

any small business owners do not fully understand the concept and benefits of add-on sales. One common example you may be familiar with includes the question, "Do you want fries with your order?" Another example is when someone purchases some type of electronic product like a remote control toy and the clerk asks "Do you need batteries for this?" The fries and batteries are considered an add-on to the sale since the customer wasn't considering purchasing these items when they first arrived at the business.

Add-Ons Add Value

Add-on sales have increased many businesses' income by as much as 30, 50, or even 75 percent, with some businesses even doubling or tripling their income. The idea of add-on sales may present an ethical dilemma if not handled appropriately. By this I mean you shouldn't be trying to sell your customers more "stuff" just for the sake of making more money. You should only be offering your customers additional services that may improve or enhance the product they are purchasing or that they may not be aware of.

For example, when a customer decides to hire you to document their wedding, they are anticipating that they will receive a three-hour (or more) video containing footage from throughout their wedding day. What they haven't considered is that it will take them three hours to watch their entire wedding video or they'll have to fast-forward through it when they want to show their friends certain parts of their wedding day. Now, if you offered your customer the option of adding a shorter highlights version of the video, where you edit down the footage to produce a 30-minute video featuring only the highlights of the day, they'll be able to show their friends and family all of the important moments from their day in only 30 minutes, and no fast-forwarding will be necessary. This is an add-on that adds value to their purchase. You could easily charge an additional $300 to $500 dollars for this option alone. This has been *the* most popular option my company has ever offered.

Possible Add-on Options to Offer

The following are more examples of some add-on options you can offer and ideas on how to present them. It helps to have examples of each one that you've already produced to show your prospective clients. It's hard to sell something they can't see. The best way to accumulate these option demos is to offer to produce one of the options that you haven't already done to your next customer for free. Offer it to them as a bonus for hiring you. For the next customer, offer them a different option or have them pick one from the list of options that you have not done yet. Before long, you'll have an example of every option you offer that you'll be able to show to prospective customers. Don't underestimate the value of doing this. Over the past five years, I've booked half of my weddings just because the client liked my childhood photo montage option *and* the fact that I can show it at their reception as well.

Childhood Photo Montage

I described this option in Chapter 6. I've found that many couples love this option and some of them like to have it shown at their reception. The best way to sell this option is to just show them one. Either they'll want it or they won't.

Love Story

This option is also described in Chapter 6. Again, show your prospective client a sample of one of these montages; either they'll want it or they won't. If you find that no one seems to want this option, it may be because they don't feel your love story videos are very good. There are training videos available to give you ideas of how to make your love stories more compelling.

Concept Video

A concept video is similar to the love story video, but without the interviews. This type of video montage involves developing a concept, theme, or script of sorts to create a unique type of music video. I recommend planning out the types of shots and what sort of theme you want the video to have. It's a good idea to choose the music you're going to use prior to shooting any video. This is another option that will sell itself when you show it to prospective clients.

Montage Presentation at Reception

This option simply involves showing one or more of the previous three options at the couple's reception. You will need to rent or buy a video projector, projector stand, and possibly a screen to do this. You will also need some type of video player, like a DVD player or one of your digital video players, and some cables to connect everything together. I will normally connect the audio output of my player to the DJ's sound system for the audio portion of the montage.

It's true that most hotels can provide this service, but the average hotel will charge the couple up to $700 for it. That's enough for couples to decide not to do it. I went ahead and purchased my own equipment, and I will charge the couple only around $350 to show the video. After I've done about a dozen of these, I will have paid for my equipment, and every projection I do after that is pure profit. This is a great opportunity to advertise my business in front of the wedding guests. This option has generated several more jobs from other couples who saw one of my montages at another wedding.

All that is required to sell this option is just to ask the couple if they would like to have their montage shown at their reception. If your montages are really entertaining to watch, there's a good chance they will want this.

Rehearsal or Rehearsal Dinner Coverage

Just as it sounds, these options involve videotaping the wedding rehearsal or the rehearsal dinner. Simply present the idea and show your prospect a sample if you have one.

Bride's Home or Groom's Home

I mentioned this option in Chapter 6, but here are a few ideas on how you can enhance this option. You could also record interviews of family members or bridesmaids during this time to make it more interesting. If you're taping the groom with his groomsmen, have them interact with each other like giving each other high fives or something. Be creative. Footage from either of these two locations will then be set to music to create a separate montage. Showing creative and well-produced montages will sell this option for you.

Additional Camera at the Ceremony or Reception

Adding another camera to your ceremony or reception coverage can dramatically improve the quality and of the video and make it more interesting to watch. Your prospective clients are used to watching movies and television programs that are filmed using more than four different camera angles, so the more camera angles you're able to add to your production, the more interesting it will be as long as every shot has a purpose for being included in the video. Since, weddings are a "one-shot" event (you don't get a second chance to capture them), having more cameras ensures that you'll get better coverage of the event. Explain to your clients some specific examples of what kinds of shots you'll be able to get with the additional camera that you couldn't get without it. For example, a third camera at the ceremony will be able to get a good shot of the groom's face during the vows that the other two cameras will not be able to get. The first camera will record the back of his head, the second camera will get the profile of his face, but the third camera will be looking right at his face, just like the bride. Show them a sample of this if you have one.

A second camera at the reception will be able to capture the guests' reactions to the best man's toast or other activities.

Wedding Highlights

I touched on this option in Chapter 6. One method I've used to sell it is by informing the client that even their good friends and family probably won't want to watch a two-and-a-half-hour wedding video, but they will watch a 30-minute video.

Honeymoon Montage

Ask your prospective client if they would like to have some of their honeymoon photos put to music at the end of their wedding video. You'll be amazed by how many will take you up on this.

Thank You Videos

Your client may be interested in recording a video "thank you" to send out to their guests, thanking them for attending. This is a unique alternative to the traditional handwritten thank you.

Printing Photos from the Video

Using Photoshop and an inkjet printer, you have the ability to print a frame of video from the wedding video. Since video is a series of photos, the average wedding video contains over 200,000 photos that the photographer may not have.

Additional Add-Ons

I've provided you with several choices to start with. One of the nice perks about this business is that it continues to change, and new ideas for add-on sales continue to be created. You may even come up with a few ideas of your own. Don't be afraid to try new things.

Chapter 15
Getting Business From Referrals

Most successful businesses today receive more than half of their business from previous customers and referrals. Customers will continue to do business with a company that has treated them well and offers them other products or services that they need. If they really like the company, they will often refer many of their friends. The wedding video business does not offer many opportunities for the prospect of repeat business from previous customers unless they happen to get married again. Therefore, you should try harder to seek referrals. Referrals may come from your previous or existing customers or they could come from another source.

Referrals From Previous or Existing Customers

The two best methods for obtaining customer referrals are to exceed your customers' expectations and to ask for referrals. Many times these two methods need to work together.

Exceeding Your Customers' Expectations

Your marketing materials, brochures, and conversations with your clients will determine your customer's expectations. If you say you're going to do something, either verbally or in writing (including your brochures), then you need to make sure you do it. That's how you meet your customer's expectations. If you don't accomplish this, you will have let your customer down and you are not likely to get any referrals. In fact, you may receive the opposite by having customers tell their friends that you don't deliver on your promises. So be sure you can deliver what you promise before you make the promise.

Now if you want referrals, you need to do better than just meeting the customer's expectations. For example, if you tell your customer that you will deliver the edited video six to eight weeks after the wedding and you are able to deliver it after only four weeks, you have exceeded their expectations. Here's another way to exceed their expectations: don't mention anything about attending the rehearsal and then show up for the rehearsal. You need to go to it anyway, as mentioned in Chapter 8; just don't let them know that you will be going. There are two major benefits to this. First, if something came up and you couldn't attend, then you don't have to worry about not delivering on your promise since you didn't say you'd come. Second, when you do show up you've exceeded their expectations by showing them how concerned you really are with doing as good a job as possible for them. After all, the photographer rarely goes to the rehearsal, so you'll look like a true professional.

When you truly have exceeded the customer's expectations, you are much more likely to get them to refer you to their friends.

Asking for Referrals

Asking for referrals is appropriate only if you were able to meet and especially exceed the customer's expectations. If you failed to do either, then you don't deserve the right to ask for referrals. When asking for a referral, ask your customer, "Do you know anyone who might benefit from my services?" If they say yes, ask for a phone number and email address. Then make sure you try to contact these people as soon as possible. The longer you wait, the less likely they are to use you. When you're able to make contact with them, tell them the name of the client who referred you to them. If they decide to hire you, then contact the referring customer and thank them for the referral. You may consider rewarding them in some way such as movie tickets or dinner at a restaurant.

Referrals from Other Sources

There are other sources you may want to seek referrals from. Here are a few examples.

Wedding Vendors

Earlier in this book, I mentioned about how important it is during the course of your work to treat other people you meet, such as other vendors, very nicely as they may refer business to you in the future. This is where that may really pay off. Each time you establish a good rapport with another wedding vendor, be sure to give them a card, or several, and ask them if they would be willing to refer you. They may tell you that they already have someone they normally refer; that's okay. Then ask them, "If, for any reason, this other person is not available for a specific job, would you consider giving me a call?"

Be sure to ask this vendor for one of their cards. Whenever you have the opportunity, refer someone to them and tell the person you referred to mention that you referred them. After this vendor has received numerous referrals from you, they'll usually start referring people to you, sometimes out of obligation.

One of the best ways to get on the referral list of the vendors you've worked with is to put together a video featuring the work they did at the wedding you worked together on. For example, if you were able to get some great footage of the flowers at the wedding; put together a video showcasing the flowers and send it to the florist. Do not charge them for doing this. If they like what they see, you should start getting referrals.

You may consider calling around or visiting other wedding vendors to see if you might be able to start up a referral relationship with them. Ask them if they would be willing to display your cards or hand them out at their place of business.

Sources Outside the Wedding Industry

Many videographers have obtained referrals from various sources not related to the wedding industry. Some sources have included networking groups, churches they belong to, present or past coworkers, and any organizations that they belong to. I'm sure you can think of even more possible sources for referrals. Don't be afraid to ask.

Offering Other Services

Many wedding videographers don't realize that they can offer other services to their past and current clients. If you are already producing photo montages for weddings, why not produce them for anniversaries, birthdays, or other occasions? Your clients may want to give a montage as a gift or to show at a party for someone they know, such as their parents. Your client may know someone else who may be interested in doing this.

If there are other services you offer, be sure to let your clients know about them. Even if they don't need those services, they may know someone who does. You never know where your next customer may come from.

Chapter 16
Handling Problems and Customer Service Issues

There will be times in your video production career when you will have problems with customers or customers with problems. Every business has them. The true measure of your success is how you handle them. This chapter is dedicated to handling some of the more common issues that may come up.

Understanding Where Problems Originate

In order for you to be able to handle problems that arise with customers, you need to know where they came from or what caused them. There are many events that can trigger a problem. Some examples include technical problems involving your equipment, unexpected events occurring during the wedding day, accidents, misunderstandings, and unrealistic expectations. Let's look at a few of the causes.

Not Meeting Customers' Expectations

This is going to sound rather obvious, but it's worth stating. Customers become unhappy when they don't receive everything they've been promised. In the previous chapter, I referred to the concept of meeting your customer's expectations. When you don't, your customer is likely to become unhappy or upset. You've failed to do what you promised you would do.

Customers Having Unrealistic Expectations

Yes, it is possible for some customers to have unrealistic expectations from time to time. For some reason, they don't understand why they can't get everything for practically nothing. Occasionally, you may have a customer who thinks that videographers should be able to capture everything that happens throughout the day no matter what. They don't realize that you can't be everywhere at the same time.

Technical Problems

There will be times when you'll have equipment that will malfunction, resulting in some missing or poor-quality audio or video. It happens to all videographers at one time or another. Some examples include audio interference while using a wireless mic and dropouts in the picture caused by the tape or a head clog in the camera.

Misunderstandings

In my opinion, this is one of the most common sources of problems or complaints. The customer believes that you promised to do certain things that you never said you would do. The customer has somehow been misled as to what they should expect to receive. Misunderstandings often turn into a "he said, she said" sort of thing. This is what makes written agreements so important. They are designed to protect both parties involved.

Unexpected Events on the Wedding Day

There may be times when something important happens on the wedding day, at a time when you're not ready to capture it. For example, the bride's father decides to go up to the DJ, grab the mic, and give an unexpected toast. Meanwhile, you were outside the room recording an interview with a guest. Even though it may not be your fault, there are ways to deal with these types of situations.

Handling Common Problems

Now that you are aware of where some of the problems come from, it's time to discuss how to handle some of these situations.

Misunderstandings and Customer's Expectations

I've combined these two problems as they are somewhat similar in nature. As I mentioned earlier, it's very important to have a signed agreement with your customers that states exactly what they can and should expect from you and, when applicable, what you are to expect from them. For example, if your customer chooses a package that includes seven hours of videotaping, that should be written in the agreement. In Chapter 7, I talked about using disclaimers in my contracts that let the customer know that I cannot be held responsible for things that are beyond my control, such as equipment malfunctions. The more thorough you are at explaining the services you will be providing, the less likely there will be misunderstandings. Just make sure you live up to your end of the bargain.

IMPORTANT TIP: Never point out to a customer what you did wrong. Let them tell you. Sometimes a big mistake to you is no big deal to them. Pointing out all of your mistakes will lower their confidence in you as a professional.

Technical Problems

In this section, I'm going to provide a few examples of specific types of technical problems. Even if you don't experience these specific problems, they may give you ideas to help you develop solutions that will resolve the problems that you do encounter.

Videotape-Related

I was taping a wedding several years ago and, as far as I could tell, everything was working fine. I had no indications whatsoever of any problems with my equipment. When it came time to edit the video, on the tape from my camera, about every 10 minutes or so, the sound would start to disappear and then the picture would become garbled. This lasted a few seconds then, the picture would clear up and the audio would return as if nothing had happened. The worst part was that all of my mics were being recorded on this tape. Fortunately, I shot the ceremony using two cameras. As I proceeded to edit the video, each time this happened, I would switch the video over to the other camera and gradually fade-in the audio from the other camera as I faded the audio from my camera out. After getting past the bad section, I would then switch both audio and video back in a similar manner. It wasn't the prettiest solution, but it worked.

Audio-Related

Over the years, I've encountered numerous problems with audio acquisition, everything from picking up a radio station through my mic to audio dropouts. To help solve these problems, I've invested in additional microphones to use as backups for when one mic fails. Between my camera's mic and the other mics I use, there's usually an alternate source of audio that I can use when one of my mics malfunctions. During the editing process, I can also check my other audio tracks to see if there's a better recording of the portion or portions I need. For example, while shooting the first dance, your DJ audio feed suddenly disappears. At the time of editing, you have two choices. You can just use the sound from your camera-mounted ambient mic or you could locate a copy of the song the couple danced to and dub it back into your video by placing it on your editing timeline.

Operator-Related

This may come as a surprise but, there have been many videographers who have missed some critical moments of the wedding day by forgetting to press the Record button on their camcorder or by thinking they already had. And often they won't discover their error until they start editing the video. You only need for this to happen once, sometimes twice, before you'll learn to make sure it doesn't happen again. I've always made it a habit to look for the letters "REC" in the viewfinder, look for the red recording light on my camera, and check to make sure the counter is moving, counting the amount of footage being shot. I may check all three of these almost every time.

Having a second camera recording during these times is a great help. You can use the footage from the second camera during the part you missed. There may be times when there isn't a second camera to fall back on. These are the moments when you are really tested as an editor to create magic.

During one of the first weddings I ever shot, somehow I missed the entire processional. Fortunately, I discovered in time that the camera was not recording and I was able to record the rest of the ceremony. But I knew I had to think of some way to fix the problem. Then I came up with a great idea. After the ceremony, when the photographer had finished shooting the portraits, I asked the bride if she would walk down the aisle again with her Dad so I could try something. She said yes. So, I walked down the aisle backwards in front of them, holding my camera low, towards the ground, while pointing it up towards the ceiling and making sure I had both of their faces in the shot. The reason for this angle is so the viewer would not be able to notice that the church was empty. That's the shot I used in place of the missing processional footage. The bride called me after she had watched the video and thanked me for such a wonderful video.

Don't Rush to Inform the Client of the Problem

This brings up a very important tip. Whenever you experience a problem during the taping of a wedding, do *not* rush to tell the client about the problem. This could mean the difference between ruining just the wedding video and ruining the entire wedding day! Brides already have enough stress to deal with on their wedding day; don't add more to it. They may come to actually hate you for doing this. If you wait to tell them long after the wedding day is over, they're much more likely to be understanding and forgiving. And, you may even be able to fix the problem without having to let them know there was one.

> **VERY IMPORTANT TIP:** If you encounter a problem during the taping of the wedding day, don't rush to inform the client. There may a way to fix it without them even knowing there was a problem. Even if you're not able to fix the problem, by waiting until long after the wedding to let them know means the worst that will have happened is you may have just ruined their wedding video as opposed to ruining their entire wedding day.

Here's how you should handle the situation. Before telling the client about the problem, first try to see if there's a way to fix the problem at some point during the wedding day, as in the previous example. If you're not able to discover a solution at the wedding, see what you can do during the editing stage. I've come up with some pretty clever fixes back in the editing studio. If you still are not able to come up with a way to fix the problem during the editing, here are a few ideas on how to tell them.

Let's say you missed the entire bouquet toss. When the client comes to pick up the video, I would tell the client that there was a problem and some of the footage didn't come out.

If you missed a part that wasn't that important, you may want to keep it to yourself. The couple probably won't miss the footage, so why bring it up?

Unexpected Events on the Wedding Day

Weeks prior to the wedding, I have my clients fill out a questionnaire letting me know what kinds of things I need to look for and be aware of on the wedding day. If they're planning any surprises, I'd like to know about them, so I can be ready to tape them. There will be times when something totally unexpected happens that my client didn't know about. As a wedding videographer, I know that I have to be ready to shoot on a moment's notice. In the event that I just can't get ready fast enough to tape this last-minute surprise, I'll inform the couple when they pick up the video. I'll tell them that there just wasn't any time for me to prepare to capture it. They usually understand in these cases.

Unique Types of Problems

The following are a few of special types of problems that might come up on occasion.

Unforeseen Delays in Completing the Video

There may be a time when something comes up that prohibits you from being able to complete your client's video by the deadline you previously specified. As soon as you discover that you will not be able to finish the video on time, you should contact the customer right away and let them know. Don't wait for them to call you, asking about their video. If your customer becomes unreasonable after you've told them, you may consider offering them some extra copies of their video at no charge or some other consideration.

Customers Wanting to Watch the Video Before Paying

In Chapter 7, I discussed issues relating to the agreement that your customer needs to sign. On the subject of payment terms, some videographers will ask to be paid in full prior to shooting the event while others will ask for partial payment prior to the event and the balance to be due when the customer receives the final edited video. If you decide that you're willing to accept the balance of the amount due upon delivery of the video, here is something you should watch out for. You may run across a customer who insists that they want to take the video home and watch it before they pay the balance due.

This can be dangerous territory. There have been instances when the customer refused to pay the balance after viewing the video, claiming that they were unhappy with the results.

To avoid being stiffed, I suggest the following. First, your contract needs to specify your payment terms. Second, you need to be firm about receiving payment before you'll release the video. If your customer is really stubborn on this issue, then I recommend offering them the option of coming into your office to watch the video. That way they will get to see it before paying the balance, but you'll still have their video. If they still want the video, they'll have to pay the balance. After they have viewed the video, they will either say the video is fine and they'll proceed to make the final payment, or they will express some sort of dissatisfaction with the video. If they are dissatisfied, then you will need to discuss with them how to remedy this so you can produce a video that meets their expectation.

This type of thing doesn't happen very often, but it's good to be aware of it in case it comes up. And, if you've done you job right, you should have very few customers who are dissatisfied with their videos. If you happen to get a customer who is unreasonably difficult to deal with, refer to the next section.

Customers Who Are Demanding

Once in a while you may come across a customer who is very demanding, the type that you just can't seem to please no matter how hard you try. If during your initial consultation with them you sense that you may have one of these customers, you may want to consider the idea of not doing business with them. You need to understand that you will not have the perfect product for everyone, and there will be some people you shouldn't do business with. You also need to be aware that it just isn't worth the stress and aggravation to conduct business with unreasonable, overly demanding people. They thrive on making your life difficult. They'll never be satisfied with your work no matter what you do. They'll never refer anyone to you. And don't be surprised if they try to get a video from you *and* want their money back. One of the key warning signs to look for is if they try to talk you into giving them a ridiculously low price for your services.

There will be customers who are only somewhat demanding. These people may ask for a few special requests, but they usually don't haggle over price. They may have special concerns, but they're usually reasonable to work with. If their demands are not too outrageous, then it may be okay to work with them. The final decision will be yours. Don't feel you have to take everyone as a client. There is a saying you should remember: "You can't please everyone." If you wind up working with a customer who tends to be unreasonably demanding, remember to be firm with them about what you will or won't do.

Tips for Resolving Difficult Situations

There will be times when you'll have a customer who is very unhappy about something that may have happened with their video. For example, if you severely messed up their video, you didn't capture a really important event during the wedding, you completed their video way past the deadline you promised, or you didn't record any sound, to name a few. And there will be times when you have no idea what your customer is upset about.

The first step is to listen to the customer talk about the problem. If they call you and they're really irate, let them vent about how unhappy they are. *Do not* interrupt them or correct them at this time; it will only make things worse. After they get everything off their chest, begin by empathizing with them. Let them know that you understand their situation and then calmly try to work out a resolution with them. If their problem was a result of something you did or forgot to do, be sure to apologize. Offer suggestions on how you can solve their problem. If they're not satisfied with any of your suggestions or you're not sure how to solve their problem, ask the customer, "What would you like me to do?" Then shut up and listen. If their suggestion seems reasonable, then tell them you'd be happy to do it. If it's not reasonable, see if you can negotiate a more reasonable solution. Your customer wants to know that you care about their problem and that you're willing to do what it takes to resolve it.

IMPORTANT TIP: Most upset customers are not mad at you, they're mad about the situation. You just happen to be in the line of fire.

You may also consider offering your customer something extra to make them feel better, such as free extra copies of the video or adding another option to the package at no charge. Use your best judgment and remember to not take it personally. Most upset customers are not mad at you, they're mad about the situation. You just happen to be in the line of fire.

Chapter 17

Keys to Maintaining Your Business

After your business is up and running, there are a few more things you need to know to ensure that your business will survive. In this chapter, I've included some suggestions for success and some traps to avoid.

Ingredients for Success

Here are a few tips to help you achieve and maintain success with your business.

Continue to Learn and Improve

One of the biggest mistakes I see videographers make is at some point in their career, they think they know everything they need to know about producing videos and how to run their business. Many of them fall into the trap of believing that since they are staying busy and none of their customers have complained about their videos, they must be doing good work and therefore have no reason to learn how to improve. Unfortunately, this industry suffers from too many videographers who feel this way. I've seen some pretty bad videos from some of these people who don't attend seminars, read books, or watch videos to learn new techniques that will allow them to keep up with their competitors. Many of the clients of our industry have received videos that were so mediocre that they did not see any reason to recommend a wedding video to their friends.

How you use your equipment will always be more important than the equipment itself. I know a videographer who uses a $3,500 camera, and his quality of work is far better than other videographers who use a $10,000 camera. It's not the tool that makes good videos, it's the person operating it along with their skill at using it. Always try to learn how to improve your skills; they will control the future of your business.

I've found that every time I learn new techniques, it renews my enthusiasm about what I do for a living. The wedding video business continues to change and evolve almost as fast as the equipment changes. There are always new ideas and ways of shooting and editing that most of us have never seen before. I strongly encourage you to continue learning as much as you can about this business for as long as you are in it. In order to keep your business thriving, you'll need to continue learning techniques for marketing, shooting, editing, selling, and running your business effectively and efficiently.

Remember the Importance of Marketing

I have always felt that marketing was more important than buying equipment. If business is slow, spending $4,000 on a new camera won't bring in more business. If you were to invest that same $4,000 in marketing, you will bring in more business. In fact, it's possible that you could earn back the $4,000 from new business and an additional $4,000 to buy that new camera. You could have the best camera in the world and be the best videographer, but if no one knows about you, you'll be out of business in the blink of an eye.

Never Stop Marketing Your Business

No matter how much business you are getting at any time, you need to always continue marketing your business. You'll discover that marketing creates results months after you've implemented it. For example, let's say your business is slow and you need business right away, so you start marketing now. You won't see results from this marketing effort for at least a few months. If you had marketed a few months earlier, when your business was busy, you would find that your business may have never slowed down at all.

I know a few videographers that have been shooting weddings for more than 10 years. Many years ago, their referral business was so good they quit marketing. They continued to thrive for several more years on referrals. Then, gradually their business began to decline, but they refused to start marketing again. A few years later, their business had declined so much that now they're doing photography instead of video.

Answering Your Phone

Many underestimate the value of simply answering your business phone. Over the years, I've booked numerous jobs because of one reason only: I was the only videographer who actually answered the phone instead of letting it go to voicemail. The clients told me how everyone else they called had an answering machine and they waited a long time for a call back. I was amazed at how many of them were surprised to actually reach a live person.

My second point on this subject has to do with how you answer the phone. Years ago, someone had told me to always answer the phone with a smile. Like many others, I thought "Who cares if I'm smiling or not? It's not like the caller can actually see me." The reality is that our body language gives away our thoughts and feelings. It tells others whether we're in a good mood or a bad mood; happy or sad, enthusiastic, or apathetic. Our body language can also tell our mind how to feel.

For example, have you ever been in a bad mood and someone comes along and smiles at you or can't stop laughing? Smiles and laughter are contagious, and before you know it, you're smiling or laughing. Once you've started smiling it's difficult to stay in a bad mood. The next time you answer the phone, try smiling before you pick up the receiver and continue smiling as long as you can. It may sound silly, but it works. Smiling while you're on the phone makes the caller feel more at ease and welcome. Don't be surprised if the caller becomes cheerful and happy. And, don't be surprised if you start feeling better yourself. Smiling is so important that I strongly encourage you to smile during all of your appointments as well.

Raising Your Prices

Starting with low prices will help stimulate business to get your business going. After you've booked your first 10 weddings, I encourage you to increase your prices by at least $100 to $150. Some videographers raise their prices $100 to $200 every year, and some raise them $50 after every three to five weddings they book. By the time you've reached your second year in business, you should have increased your prices by at least $200. You may be wondering why this is so important. The two most important benefits of raising prices are the ability to stay in business and creating a professional image.

Staying in Business

In order to keep you motivated to stay in this business, you need to be able to earn a living and take care of your family. More than half of the videographers shooting weddings don't realize that they make less per hour than most fast-food restaurant employees. I've always wondered why they would want to put themselves through all of the stress of running a business to make less than $5 an hour. Many of them don't know how to determine how much they are really making, so they continue doing what they've been doing. This will eventually put them out of business.

HELPFUL TIP: If you want to see how much you are making on an hourly basis, go to www.provideotraining.com and download a free copy of the "Estimating your hourly wage worksheet."

The wedding video business has many overhead costs that people forget about. The technology changes rapidly, and you need to factor in the costs of upgrading your equipment when the time comes. There's also the cost of advertising, insurance, transportation to and from the events, blank tapes and DVDs, cases and printing for the tapes and DVDs, education to keep you up to date on the latest trends, software programs, and more. These costs can add up to $25 an hour or more for every hour you spend working on someone's video.

Videographers also tend to forget to include all of the time they spend meeting with clients and working on their wedding video. For example, when you add a few hours for the initial consultation, 5 to 10 hours of videotaping on the wedding day and the 20 to 40 hours editing it, your average wedding video may well have 50 hours of time invested into it.

Let's say you'd like to make $50,000 per year of net income for yourself, and your total overhead costs are $30,000 per year including equipment purchases. You would have to gross $80,000 a year to reach your goal. The average videographer may book 30 weddings a year. 30 weddings a year times 50 hours equals 1,500 hours of labor. $80,000 divided by 1,500 hours equals $53.33 per hour. $53.33 times 50 hours for one wedding equals $2,666.67. So, you would have to charge $2,667 per wedding based on 30 weddings per year in order to net $50,000 in income. If you only book 25 weddings then the price per wedding will be more. Now you can see why you'll want to raise prices.

Generating a Professional Image

This may be a little hard to believe, but charging more for your services will make you appear more professional. For example, if you had a problem with your heart and required heart surgery, would you hire a surgeon that only charges $500? Probably not. After receiving a quote like that you'd be asking questions like what kind of experience does he have, where did he get his training or go to school, what are his qualifications, and do I want him to operate on me? You more likely to perceive a surgeon charging $10,000 to be more of a professional than the one charging $500.

In my second year of business, I raised my prices by $200. I booked somewhat fewer weddings than the previous year but my income was higher. In my third year, I raised them by $200 again. My bookings went down a little more but my income increased even more. In my fourth year, I raised them by $500. This time, my bookings doubled and so did my income.

If it makes you feel more comfortable, you could raise your prices by $50 after every five weddings you book. The more weddings you shoot, the more experienced you'll become and the better your videos will look, therefore you'll be worth the higher fee.

WARNING: Ignoring the importance of making a profit has forced thousands of entrepreneurs out of business.

Traps to Avoid

No one ever said that owning or running a business was easy. There will be some bumps along the way. There will also be some major obstacles and pitfalls that you'll need to avoid in order to remain in business. I've included a few of them here.

Always Buying the Latest Equipment

Some videographers find themselves always wanting to buy the latest and greatest equipment to keep up with the technology. I have to warn you against doing this. While it is true that they continue to develop better cameras, mics, computers, and software, you don't need to have the newest equipment to be successful in this business. Each and every equipment purchase you make needs to be carefully evaluated to be sure that it is truly necessary and will pay for itself in the shortest time possible.

Be Careful of What You Promise

Never promise a customer something unless you are 100 percent sure you can deliver. You may be setting yourself up for a potential lawsuit.

Booking Multiple Weddings on the Same Day

Early in my wedding video career, ambition pushed me into booking more than one wedding on the same day on several occasions. This often involved shooting one wedding in the morning and another in the late afternoon or evening. I quickly learned what a bad idea that was.

First, you have to have fully charged and fresh batteries for all of your equipment by the time you begin taping the second wedding. If you just exhausted your camera's batteries shooting the first wedding, how will you recharge them for the second?

Second, videotaping weddings is a very physically and mentally demanding job. By the time you've finished taping the first wedding, you're exhausted and you have to prepare to do it all over again. Personally, I believe it's not really fair to the client having the second wedding since it will be hard for you to be at the top of your game when you're that tired.

On one occasion, I hired a second crew to shoot another wedding that was scheduled to start during the middle of a wedding I would be shooting. The main concerns I had were wondering if they would show up and show up on time and how would their shooting style and quality of work compare to mine. I decided later that I no longer desired to have the added stress of dealing with a second wedding.

Booking Too Many Weddings Too Fast

The previous section brings me to a really important topic I need to address. Most videographers who experience early success become tempted to overbook themselves too soon, taking on as many weddings as they can collect deposits for. While the extra money is great, it can lead to serious problems in the near future.

The process starts when, through your marketing efforts and referrals, you have a surge of customers wanting to hire you to videotape their weddings. It feels like you've become really popular really fast. It becomes hard to resist the opportunity to take a check. So, you keep saying yes and writing another wedding in your appointment book. The next thing you know, summer is over, and you have accumulated a rather large collection of weddings that need to be edited.

With all of the demands on your time from meeting with prospective clients and current clients, answering the phone calls, all of the preparation that goes into preparing for each and every wedding shoot, and trying to run a business, you have begun to get behind in your editing. Weddings that used to take less than a week to edit are now taking two or more weeks to complete because of all of the new demands on your time. Before you know it, you're now two months behind, then three months, then four. Your customers are starting to call you, asking when their video will be finished. The stress level is increasing, you're working 12, 14, 16 hours a day, seven days a week trying to catch up. You no longer can find time to spend with your family or friends, and you start having to miss important occasions so you can edit. You're beginning to feel the effects of wedding burnout.

The day comes when you realize that not only are you six or even eight months behind on your editing but that at this pace you may never be able to catch up. Your customers are calling you practically every day, wondering where their video is, and they're starting to tell their friends they can't believe how long it's taking. Instead of getting referrals, your clients are starting to tell people why they shouldn't hire you. Now your bookings are starting to decline as Internet chat rooms are filling up with more complaints about your company's turnaround time. Before long, it seems like no one wants to hire you because they feel it's not worth the wait, so they go elsewhere. Now you're starting to wonder whether you still want to continue working in this business.

I've personally witnessed this process both firsthand and by watching numerous other videographers go through it. Many of them are no longer working in the wedding video business. Once you've begun accepting too many weddings, this *will* happen to you if you don't stop it before it's too late. There is a simple solution to this problem. It requires that you learn when and how to say no to business. I know it's not as easy as it sounds, but here's a tip that should help you. Raise your prices. By raising your prices, you will reach a point when you will start seeing a slowdown in your bookings. When your prices hit a point where you are booking only as many weddings as you can edit while maintaining a reasonable turnaround time, then you can start slowing down the rate of your price increases. If you want more free time in your schedule, raise them a little more.

You need to keep your workload under control in order to avoid wedding burnout and creating very dissatisfied customers. After all, didn't you get into this business so you could enjoy your work?

Failing to Seek Help

One of the leading causes for small business failures is the inability of the business owner to seek outside help. This can be remedied by reading books, listening to CDs or tapes, watching instructional videos, attending seminars, or by seeking the advice of someone with the right experience.

Congratulations

There was a lot of information, but you made it through. If you haven't already started your business, it's time to get going. By now, you should have enough information to get your business off the ground.

If you found this book to be extremely helpful with your video business, drop me a line at info@provideotraining.com. I'd love to hear your success story.

I wish you all the success with your new venture.

Glossary

ambient sound all of the natural sounds that can be heard from the existing environment, including any sounds that may have been reflected off surrounding walls; for example, all of the sounds you hear in the church, from people talking to baby's crying or doors being closed—all of the sounds that exist in that room or space

altar structure upon which offering are offered, usually located at the front of the church

audio another name for sound

audio channel a source, path, or track for sound to be recorded, monitored, or played back. A stereo sound source contains two audio channels or tracks.

audio feed a connection to an output jack of a soundboard or audio mixer that enables another device to receive the same sound as the sound output (final mix) that will be sent to the main speakers of the sound system

audio level a setting that controls the volume level of the sound

audio mixer a device used for controlling the volume levels from multiple sound sources independently of each other. With the audio mixer, all of the sources can be mixed down to one or two audio channels for recording.

authored DVD a DVD that contains a custom menu with chapter points that you determine at the time of authoring. Most DVD movies sold in stores are authored DVDs. These DVDs are created using a computer.

back camera the camera located at the back of the church

battery belt a set of battery cells attached to belt that you wear around your waist. These are used to provide power for lights and cameras.

CCD a type of computer chip that converts images into electrical information that can be recorded onto electronic media

close-up a shot derived by zooming in on a subject as much as the camera will allow or filling the camera's frame with someone's entire face

cross-dissolve (dissolve) a transition where one scene fades out while another fades in

cross-fade decreasing the volume of one audio clip as you increase the volume of another audio clip

cut edit an edit where one video clip ends and the next clip begins without any transition between them

cutaway shot footage of something other than what the primary camera is focused on, used to cover up unwanted footage or to connect two disjointed video clips. It is usually followed by returning to the primary camera's footage. Also referred to as B roll.

dissolve (cross-dissolve) a transition where one scene fades out while another fades in

DJ disc jockey, the person who plays the music and makes the announcements at a reception if there isn't a band

downtime periods of time during the wedding day when there's nothing happening that warrants taping, such as during the meal

dropouts (audio or video) parts of a videotape where the audio or video disappear for a period of time

dutch-angle a type of video shot where the top of the camera is tilted up to 40 degrees to the left or the right, making the image appear crooked

DVD burner a device used to record information onto a blank DVD

DVD recorder a name commonly used to refer to a standalone DVD burner that operates similar to a VCR while recording information or video onto a blank DVD

edit master a copy of the final edited video stored on a videotape, disc, or some other type of media other than a computer hard drive. In some cases, edit masters are used to create copies of the video for the customer.

establishing shot the opening shot of a scene or a video that shows the viewer where the following events will be taking place

fade to black transitioning from a scene to a black screen using a simple dissolve. Also called fade out.

fade from black transitioning from black to a new scene using a simple dissolve. Also called fade in.

fictitious name using a business name that is different than your own name

FireWire Commonly used to describe a type of connection and cable for connecting two digital components such as a camera and a VCR, allowing the transfer of information from one unit to the other while keeping it in a digital format. Sometimes referred to as an IEEE 1394 cable or connection.

focus the part of the camera's lens that controls the sharpness of the images being recorded

footage a video clip or clips

front camera the camera located at the front of the church

head clog a loss of video signal as a result of dirt on the video head of a video recorder during recording or playback

high-angle shot a shot where the camera is positioned over the head of the camera operator while pointed slightly downward to provide a view of the activity from above

high definition a newer standard of video containing up to 1,028 lines of resolution compared to the 300 to 400 lines of resolution on traditional analog televisions. Because of the increased resolution, the picture quality is much sharper than that of traditional analog TV sets. Often referred to as High Def or HD.

in focus the image in the camera being sharp, crisp, and clear

iris the part of the camera's lens that controls the amount of light that will be allowed into the camera

line level the voltage level of an audio signal. This level is a substantially higher voltage (and volume) level than a mic-level signal. If you send a line-level signal to a mic-level input, it will overpower the input, causing distortion.

linear dub recording video or audio from one source to another media, starting from the beginning and continuing to the end

long-form edit an edited version of the wedding video that includes most of the raw footage and all of the activities recorded on the wedding day

low-angle shot a type of video shot where the camera is positioned near the ground while pointed upward to provide a view of the activity from below

MC (master of ceremonies) the person in charge of coordinating the activities and making announcements at a reception, usually the DJ

medium shot a shot derived by zooming approximately halfway between a close-up and a wide-angle shot, in the middle of the camera's zoom range. When videotaping people, the shot will consist of the top half of their body from their waist to the top of their head

mic nickname for microphone

mic level the voltage level of an audio signal. This level is a substantially lower voltage (and volume) level than a line-level signal. If you send a mic-level signal to a line-level input, it will have such a low level that you may not be able to hear it.

montage (photo or video) a series of different clips or images that are put together, usually with music, to create a video with a smooth flow

MPEG-2 a compression algorithm that compresses video into smaller file sizes. This allows up to two hours of video to be put onto one DVD disc. There is a small amount of picture quality sacrificed in doing this.

out of focus when the image in the camera is blurry and lacks detail

overhead the expenses associated with the day-to-day operations of your business, such as insurance, rent, office supplies, blank media for recording, and wages paid to employees

pacing the flow of the video from beginning to end. It may be fast, slow, or a combination of both. Pacing often refers to the length of time used to transition from one scene to another throughout the video.

pan turning the camera horizontally while keeping the camera the same distance from the ground

picture-in-picture two video clips displayed on a video monitor at the same time with the entire frame of video from one clip inserted over a portion of the video from another clip. Usually, it covers one corner of the other video clip on the display monitor.

podium (reader podium) a stand often used in wedding ceremonies for scripture readings

processional the first part of a wedding ceremony when the entire wedding party comes down the aisle, concluding after the bride has reached the altar or the front of the church and the music has stopped

production monitor a video monitor designed to accurately display the color, brightness, and detail information from a video source

prosumer a category of electronic equipment (usually video-related) that exists between the consumer-level products and the professional-level products. This category may include items at the top of the consumer-level and the bottom of the professional-level products.

push using the telephoto mechanism within the camera's lens to bring the subject in closer, making it appear larger. Also referred to as zooming in.

pull using the telephoto mechanism within the camera's lens to move the subject farther away, making it appear smaller. Also referred to as zooming out.

raw footage the original videotape recording made using a camera or camcorder prior to being edited

real-time recording a recording where the recording time will be the same as the actual length of the program being recorded

recessional the last part of a wedding ceremony when the bride and groom start back up the aisle to exit the back of the church, concluding after all of the wedding party and family have walked back up the aisle and exited the church as well

reseller's permit a permit issued by your local or regional government entity responsible for collecting sales tax. The permit gives you the legal right to sell products or services that are considered to be taxable by your governing authority.

reveal shot a shot where the camera pulls back to reveal more of the scenery. Same as a pull or zooming out.

shoot the act of going out on location to videotape something

shooting videotaping

short-form edit an edited version of the wedding video that includes just the highlights of the wedding day, usually less than an hour in length

shutter the part of the camera's lens that opens and closes, allowing an image to be captured onto a frame of video

shutter speed the amount of time the shutter will remain open while capturing an image

soundboard another name for an audio mixer, used for mixing and fading in or fading out various sound sources

split-screen two video clips displayed on a video monitor side by side at the same time

sync nickname for synchronize

time-compression an editing technique where portions of the video are removed to shorten the video without sacrificing important content

timeline one of the windows used in a video editing software program where video clips are placed in the order they are to be shown. Most of the editing is done within this window.

transition (video transition) a type of effect, placed between two different video clips, that lets the viewer know we are leaving one scene or shot and going to another

unauthored DVD a DVD that is created using a standalone DVD recorder. These DVDs usually contain generic menus that you cannot customize.

VCR video cassette recorder, usually referring to the VHS format. Sometimes referred to as VTR.

video capture card a card in a computer that enables a video source to be connected to a computer for the purpose of converting video to computer files that can be edited in a video editing software program

VTR videotape recorder, meaning any tape recorder used for recording video. Often used interchangeably with VCR.

white balance an adjustment to the camera that provides the camera with a reference point as to what the color white should look like under a specific lighting condition. Once the camera is calibrated to the current lighting environment, the camera will automatically adjust all other colors of the image accordingly.

white balancing the act of adjusting the camera's white balance for the lighting environment of the shooting location

wide-angle shot a shot derived by zooming out from a subject as much as the camera will allow, showing as much as possible

zoom the part of the camera's lens that allows you to enlarge the image, making it appear closer, or shrink the image, making it appear farther away

zoom in using the telephoto mechanism within the camera's lens to bring the subject in closer, making it appear larger. Also referred to as a push.

zoom out using the telephoto mechanism within the camera's lens to move the subject farther away, making it appear smaller. Also referred to as a pull.

Additional Resources

Recommended Training Videos

Camera Command by RAVAS Partners

Advanced Broadcast Camera Techniques, Volumes 1 and 2 by John Cooksey

Digital Lighting Magic by John Cooksey

Sounds Like Creative Video by Randy Stubbs

Ordinary to Extraordinary by Randy Stubb

Creating Graphics Clients Love, Volumes 1 and 2 by Lance Gray

Guide to Adobe Premiere by Luisa Winters

Web Sites

www.provideotraining.com

www.dv.com

Magazines

DV

Event DV

Videography

Videomaker

Index

LIGHTING FOR DIGITAL VIDEO & TELEVISION, 2ND EDITION
JOHN JACKMAN

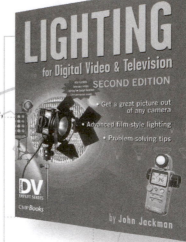

Get a complete course in video and television lighting from a seasoned pro. Detailed illustrations and real-world examples demonstrate proper equipment use, safety issues, troubleshooting, and staging techniques. This new edition features an 8-page full-color insert and new chapters on interview setups, as well as low-budget lighting setups on location.

$39.95, softcover, 256 pages, ISBN 1-57820-251-5

PRODUCING GREAT SOUND FOR DIGITAL VIDEO, 2ND EDITION
JAY ROSE

Produce compelling audio with this arsenal of real-world techniques to use from pre-production through mix. Includes step-by-step tutorials, tips, and tricks you can use to make great tracks with any computer or software. Audio CD contains sample tracks, demos, and diagnostic tools.

$44.95, softcover with audio CD, 428 pages, ISBN 1-57820-208-6

COLOR CORRECTION FOR DIGITAL VIDEO
STEVE HULLFISH & JAIME FOWLER

Use desktop tools to improve your storytelling, deliver critical cues, and add impact to your video. Beginning with a clear, concise description of color and perception theory, this full-color book shows you how to analyze color correction problems and solve them—whatever NLE or plugin you use. Refine your skills with tutorials that include secondary and spot corrections and stylized looks.

$49.95, full-color softcover with CD-ROM, 202 pages, ISBN 1-57820-201-9

VIDEO SHOOTER
STORYTELLING WITH DV, HD AND HDV CAMERAS
BARRY BRAVERMAN

Create a compelling visual story for any project with this engaging guide. Industry veteran Barry Braverman draws on over 20 years of experience, including work on *National Geographic* specials, to illustrate the complete range of skills required to capture great images. Key topics include equipment selection, set-up, camera operation, shooting techniques, lighting, and audio.

$44.95, full-color softcover with DVD, 256 pages, ISBN 1-57820-289-2

DESIGNING DVD MENUS
MICHAEL BURNS AND GEORGE CAIRNS

Design DVD menus with that cool, professional edge. Begin by cutting through the jargon and technical issues; then analyze an array of projects to see how to use animation, picture-within-picture, background movie clips, and audio and imaging effects to create stunning titles, menu screens, transitions, and interactive features. This book includes 500+ color illustrations with a showcase gallery of great DVD interface designs.

$44.95, softcover, 192 pages, ISBN 1-57820-259-0

PHOTOSHOP CS FOR NONLINEAR EDITORS, 2ND EDITION
RICHARD HARRINGTON

Use Photoshop CS to generate characters, correct colors, and animate graphics for digital video. You'll grasp the fundamental concepts and master the complete range of Photoshop tools through lively discourse, full-color presentations, and hands-on tutorials. The companion DVD contains 120 minutes of video lessons, tutorial media, and plug-ins.

$54.95, softcover with DVD, 310 pages, ISBN 1-57820-237-X

What's on the DVD

In addition to a sample agreement form and questionnaire, the DVD contains sample clips (excerpts) of the following:

Photo montage

Love Story

From the Ceremony

Processional
Scripture Reading
Sermon
Vows
Rings
Unity Candle lighting
Cord/Veil
Kiss & Recessional
Post-Ceremony montage
Outdoor wedding
An example of Time-compression

From the Reception

Wedding Party Intro
Mealtime entertainment
Toast
First Dance
Father-Bride dance
Wedding Party dance
Cake-cutting
Honeymoon dance
Open dancing
Bouquet Toss
Garter Toss
Interview

Updates

Want to receive e-mail updates for *The Wedding Video Handbook?* Visit our web site www.cmp-books.com/maillist and select from the desired categories. You'll automatically be added to our preferred customer list for new product announcements, special offers, and related news.

Your e-mail address will not be shared without your permission, so sign up today!